The Crack in the Picture Window

by JOHN KEATS
illustrated by DON KINDLER
Houghton Mifflin Company, Boston
The Riverside Press, Cambridge

THE CRACK IN THE

PICTURE WINDOW

Fourth printing April 1957

The lines from *The House and the Art of Its Design* by Robert
Woods Kennedy are reprinted by permission of the Reinhold
Publishing Corporation; the lines from *Survival Through Design*
by Richard Neutra are reprinted by permission of the Oxford
University Press; the lines from *The Expanding Environment*
by E. A. Gutkind are reprinted by permission of the Freedom
Press; the lines from *Town and Countryside* by Thomas Sharp
are reprinted by permission of the Oxford University Press.
The Riverside Press · Cambridge, Massachusetts
Printed in the U.S.A.

Acknowledgments

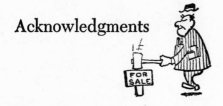

I OWE a debt to the people who live in housing developments, who unwittingly wrote this thing for me. And to Mr. Tom Donnelley of the *Washington Daily News*, who named John Drone; to Mr. Frederick A. Gutheim for thoughtful suggestion and the use of his definitive library; to Mr. Robert Jones, Miss Elizabeth O'Malley, Mr. Harold Taubin, Mr. Harold Mendelsohn and Mr. Harold Keats for expert advice in the fields of social work, community planning, sociology and real-estate finance; to John and Martha McLeod, Evert and June Clark, Muriel and Don Kindler for their patient (and by now deafened) ears. And first and last, I owe a debt to my lady wife, who came to loathe John Drone.

Contents

Introduction

Welcome to the Inquest

FOR LITERALLY NOTHING DOWN—other than a simple two per cent and a promise to pay, and pay, and pay until the end of your life—you too, like a man I'm going to call John Drone, can find a box of your own in one of the fresh-air slums we're building around the edges of America's cities. There's room for all in any price range, for even while you read this, whole square miles of identical boxes are spreading like gangrene throughout New England, across the Denver prairie, around Los Angeles, Chicago, Washington, New York, Miami—everywhere. In any one of these new neighborhoods, be it in Hartford or Philadelphia, you can be certain all other houses will be precisely like yours, inhabited by people whose age, income, number of children, problems, habits, conversation, dress, possessions and perhaps even blood type are also precisely like yours. In any one of these neighborhoods it is possible to make enemies of the folks next door with unbelievable speed. If you buy a small house, you are assured your children will leave you perhaps even sooner than they should, for at once they will learn never to associate home with pleasure. In short, ladies and gentlemen, we offer here for your inspection facts relative to today's housing developments—developments conceived in error, nurtured by greed, corroding everything they touch. They destroy established cities and trade patterns, pose dangerous problems for the areas they invade, and actually drive mad myriads of housewives shut up in them.

These facts are well known to responsible economists, sociologists, psychiatrists, city managers and bankers, and certainly must be suspected by the people who live in the suburban developments, yet there's no end in sight to the construction. Indeed, Washington's planners exult whenever a contractor vomits up five thousand new houses on a rural tract that might better have remained in hay, for they see in this little besides thousands of new sales of labor, goods and services. Jobs open for an army of bulldozer operators, carpenters, plasterers, plumbers, electricians, well-diggers, bricklayers, truck drivers, foremen and day laborers. Then come the new householders, followed by their needs. A shopping center and supermarket are hurriedly built, and into this pours another army of clerical and sales personnel, butchers, bakers, janitors, auto dealers, restaurateurs, waitresses, door-to-door salesmen, mail carriers, rookie cops, firemen, schoolteachers, medicine men of various degrees— the whole ruck and stew of civilization's auxiliaries. Thus, with every new development, jobs are born, money is earned, money is spent, and pretty soon everyone can afford a new television set, and Washington calls this prosperity.

That such prosperity is entirely material, possibly temporary and perhaps even illusory, causes little concern at present. It's money, isn't it? Well, maybe it is and maybe it isn't. A later chapter will show whether any development householder really owns the house he thinks he's bought—whether he owns the things he uses. It's sufficient at this point to suggest the rooftrees of the nation's Levittowns are held up by levitation.

Meanwhile, let's step back in time to consider the history of today's housing developments:

The first good intentions which pave our modern Via Dolorosa were laid at war's end. Conscious of the fact that some 13,000,000 young men risked disfigurement, dismemberment and death in circumstances not of their choosing, a grateful nation decided to show its appreciation to the survivors. The GI Bill of Rights was enacted, and one of the articles provided an incentive for bankers to assume low-interest mortgages on houses purchased by veterans. The deal was, the bankers could recover a certain guaranteed sum from the government in event of the veteran's default. The real-estate boys read the Bill, looked at one another in happy amazement, and the dry, rasping noise they made rubbing their hands together could have been heard as far away as Tawi Tawi. Immediately, thanks to modern advertising, movable type, radio, television and other marvels, the absurdity was spread—and is still spread—that the veteran should own his home.

There was never the slightest justification for this nonsense. Never in the last 180 years of United States history was there an indication that a young man entering civil life from childhood or war should thereupon buy a house.

It is and has always been the nature of young people to be mobile. Rare indeed is the man whose life is a straight arrow's-flight from the classroom to the job he'll hold until he dies. Many a retiring corporate officer put in his early

years driving a bread truck, then had a fling at a little un-
successful business of his own, then wandered into the door-
to-door sale of cemetery lots before catching on at the
buttonworks he was one day to direct. Owning property
implies a certain permanence—precisely that quality a bright
young man should, and does, lack. A young man should be
mobile until he finds his proper path. A man with a house
is nailed to its floor.

The housing article in the GI Bill, however, opened vast
vistas. Not only was there a government guarantee to be
had, but there was also land to be sold, and since the veteran
had been led both by private and government propaganda
to believe he should own his home, the remaining consideration in the hard, practical minds of the real-estate men
was how much house could be offered for how little money.
Or, to put it in the more usual way, how little house could
be offered for how much money. Cost became the sole criterion of the first postwar house, and the first economy was
in space.

The typical postwar development operator was a man
who figured how many houses he could possibly cram onto
a piece of land and have the local zoning board hold still
for it. Then he whistled up the bulldozers to knock down
all the trees, bat the lumps off the terrain, and level the
ensuing desolation. Then up went the houses, one after another, all alike, and none of those built immediately after
the war had any more floor space than a moderately-priced,
two-bedroom apartment. The dining room, the porch, the
basement, and in many cases the attic, were dispensed with
and disappeared from the American scene. The result was a
little box on a cold concrete slab containing two bedrooms,
bath, and an eating space the size of a broom closet tucked

between the living room and the tiny kitchen. A nine-by-twelve rug spread across the largest room wall to wall, and there was a sheet of plate glass in the living-room wall. That, the builder said, was the picture window. The picture it framed was of the box across the treeless street. The young Americans who moved into these cubicles were not, and are not, to know the gracious dignity of living that their parents knew in the big two- and three-story family houses set well back on grassy lawns off the shady streets of, say, Watertown, New York. For them and their children, there would be only the box on its slab. The Cape Cod Rambler had arrived.

It was inevitable that the development house was looked upon as an expedient by the young purchasers. It was most certainly not the house of their dreams, nor was the ready-made neighborhood a thing to make the soul sing. It was, simply, the only thing available. They had no choice—they couldn't afford to build their house, nor were they given a choice of architecture. Instead, they were offered a choice between a house they didn't much want and the fantastic rents that bobbed to the surface as soon as the real-estate lobby torpedoed rent control. The development house was the only living space on the market priced just within the means of the young veterans.

It is still a maxim with responsible land agents that you should never purchase a home in which you do not intend to dwell for at least ten years. Moreover, they'll say, a house in which you have no equity cannot be considered an investment. Despite these truths, houses were bought on the assumption they would serve only as brief campsites on life's wilderness trail, and incredibly enough, the government in the past two years has given encouragement to this singular point of view. With government blessing, purchasers are now being advised that buying a new house is like buying a new car. Old one too small for the growing family? Trade your old home in and buy a new one, the government suggests, meanwhile helping the developers to continue their dirty work in order that prosperity's bubble doesn't burst.

The first veterans' developments set a pattern for the builders. They sold the first houses like hotcakes, so they've been making hotcakes ever since. Today's new houses differ from those of 1947 only insofar as the materials are better and the workmen have now mastered their jobs. The basic living problems are unchanged—they're built right in. These problems will remain unchanged unless the whole construction pattern changes; until a housing development becomes something more than just a lot of houses.

First of all, a housing development cannot be called a community, for that word implies a balanced society of men, women and children wherein work and pleasure are found and the needs of all the society's members are served. Housing developments offer no employment and as a general rule lack recreational areas, churches, schools, or other cohesive influences.

A second present and future national danger lies in the fact that developments are creating stratified societies of singular monotony in a nation whose triumph to date has depended on its lack of a stratified society, on the diversity of its individuals. Yet today it is possible to drive through the various developments that surround one of our cities and tell at a glance the differing social strata.

Here is the $10,000 development—two bedrooms, low-priced cars, average income $75 a week after taxes, three children, average food budget $25 weekly; jobs vary from bus driver to house painter. Here is the $13,950 house—three bedrooms, available to foremen and successful newspapermen, medium-priced cars, two and a half children per average home; men's shoes cost $12 to $20 at this level. Next is the $17,450 split level, especially designed for split personalities, upper-medium cars; liquor bill is $25 weekly; inmates take fly-now-pay-later air rides to Europe.

The appearance of several square miles of new housing units in a once rural area adjacent to a city normally brings about a violent clash of interests. The young new householders, conscious only of their unmet needs, are intolerant of the political milieu they've invaded. Indeed, if there was any cohesive force acting on typical development householders, it would be that of hatred. Well might they form a sort of mutual loathing society where the first target of their wrath is the builder, the second, the community around them.

For its part, the invaded community eyes the newcomers with something less than wild enthusiasm. The administrative problems handed a county government by the sudden appearance of several thousand new families are enough to make a strong man blench. And, when the guts of a city are deserted by a middle class that flocks to the suburbs, the tax problems created for the city fathers are even more frightening.

In any discussion of housing developments, however, we must first and last consider that poor devil, the householder. John Drone did not know it when he signed the deed, but appalling human tensions were a condition of the sale. Now these tensions are a tightening, knotted cord about his temples as he stands there on tiptoes, his hands tied, struggling for balance on the sharp roof of the house he may not own, nostril-deep in swirling debt.

The Crack in the Picture Window

1. This Is the Ace That Drone Drew

"We cut the deck and drew an ace, '42 will set the pace."—University of Pennsylvania Class of 1942 cheer

THE JUBAL EARLY HOMES, government-rented to veterans only, was a dilapidated set of jerry-built barracks situated in a near-swamp on the outskirts of Alexandria, Virginia, and here, in the mud and in the smell of sour milk and dirty diapers, lived John and Mary Drone with their two infant children. Through their fiberboard walls they could easily hear the racket of near-by National Airport and the constant roar of trucks on Route One. These sounds came through as a sort of background to the lighter, more immediate tones of their neighbors' radios, cursing, love-making and crying babies. It wasn't precisely Heaven, but the Drones at first were glad to have one of the apartments and Mary bravely tried to make theirs into something resembling a home.

She fought her losing battle for nearly a year, but the end came the day she saw a roach grazing on her baby's face. With a little cry of horror, Mary snatched up the sleeping child, and as she did so, other roaches scuttered deeper into the folds of the crib blankets. Mary was still crying when John came home from his government clerical job that night.

"We're simply going to have to move," she told him, sobbing. "I've tried and I've tried, but I can't stand this any longer. Look at it," she said, her voice reaching exactly the same note she would have recognized in the voices of her neighbors' wives. "Look outside. Mud and clotheslines and. . .

"I," she said, "I . . . I . . . when I saw those roaches in the *crib*, I was so upset I forgot the time and I missed my washing period at the machines and now your wash didn't get done and you'll have to wear that shirt again tomorrow."

John folded his arms about her. Mary clung to him and he looked tenderly into her tear-blurred face.

"I guess," he murmured, "I better get some more roach paste."

"Roach paste!" she screamed, tearing loose and looking for the first time at the man she married. "Roach paste! You better get us a place to live, if you want me to live with you. Until then, I'm going back to Philadelphia with Chip and the baby and stay in mother's apartment."

Slowly, John Drone faced up to the ultimatum. They'd have to move. But where? And to what? He drew the minimum government salary and the modest Jubal Early Homes rent was all he could afford. He lacked the guts to throw up his U.S. job and its lifetime security to seek better work in private industry. He didn't think he should take the chance—not with a wife and two children to support. Furthermore, as the Drones knew only too well, there was no vacant rental property within their means within thirty miles of Washington, D.C. Not in 1948. For that matter, there was no vacant rental property *beyond* their means—

there were long waiting lists even for the $250-a-month apartments. As it was, the Drones had lived in a loft over a one-car garage for nine months, waiting for their names to arrive at the top of the Jubal Early list.

All this might suggest there was a housing shortage in and around the Federal City. But to the landlords, those people best in position to know, there was no housing shortage. The trouble seemed to them simply that too many people were occupying too much space. Mr. Rufus Lusk, a Washington real-estate lobbyist, explained this quite clearly to fascinated Congressmen.

Too many people, he warned, were making too much money. People who should be doubling up in rooming houses were, instead, using their war-swollen salaries to rent more space than they should, by rights, enjoy. Three and four government girls were getting together to rent a large—two- or three-bedroom—apartment. If only some means could be found to push these young ladies back into the woodwork of the old brownstone rooming houses, the so-called housing shortage would disappear, he said. It was just like the meat shortage. The only reason steaks were scarce was that too many people who should be eating hamburger were, instead, eating steaks. Hence, the people who should be eating steaks couldn't find them in the markets.

Moreover, Mr. Lusk explained, the real sufferers in the housing dilemma were the landlords. Everyone was making more money, labor costs were rising, cost of materials was going up, but landlords lay helpless in the grip of rent control. Just remove rent control, he argued, and the landlords would mercifully be freed from an unjust discrimination. There would be some slight, momentary, upward trends to rents, to be sure. But then, perhaps those government secretaries would stream back into the old brownstones and rents would "level off" and, meanwhile, the shortage would have solved itself.

To John and Mary Drone, however, there seemed to be a real housing shortage in that they could have afforded adequate quarters at the controlled rent, but that no such quarters were available. In fact, the situation was to get worse before it improved—if it has improved—and a slight digression at this point will help us see the Drones' predicament. It was one in which hundreds of thousands of John Drones across the nation found themselves.

Bit by bit, Mr. Lusk and other real-estate lobbyists chiseled away at rent control until, by 1951, there was no control on housing never previously offered on the rental market, and at long last the landlords had their innings. And here, according to a Senate investigating committee report, is how the game was played from then on:

Veterans' families were offered rental space in "garages, coal sheds, chicken coops, barns, tool sheds, granaries and smokehouses. Such hovels are merely gestures of contempt toward those who are desperate enough to take anything which is offered . . . Structures with no water available, heating facilities so bad that bottled drinks will freeze in the same room with a large stove, no sanitary toilet facilities, primitive food storage, no sinks, cardboard windowpanes and paper walls, cannot in 1951 be regarded as housing."

Moreover, the Senate found, the new, uncontrolled rental prices "range from a commonplace 100% to 500% per month over rentals previously obtained for comparable quarters."

Senator Thomas Hennings of Missouri summed it up. He

said, ". . . the plain fact of the matter is that the unscrupulous landlords who are extorting outrageous rents for dilapidated, filthy hovels are doing so, in most cases, strictly within the limits of the law."

That Senate report was not confined to Washington any more than it was to Kentucky. It was a report on the state of the Union's lack of rental housing. It was a government report on another victory for blind greed, a victory obtained with the help of Congress itself. Meanwhile, huge new apartment projects were springing up around the edges of American cities, and rentals for their adequate quarters stretched the limits of human imagination. In those built in the Washington area, one-room efficiency flats were renting for $110 a month.

Seen in this perspective, it would appear that John and Mary Drone in 1948 were relatively lucky to have found a draughty, ugly, roach-infested, one-bedroom apartment of their own. By government regulation of their housing project, they shouldn't have had that—for the regulations said two children called for a two-bedroom unit. Their second child, however, hadn't been conceived when they first signed the waiting list and, furthermore, consideration of relative good fortune was lost on Mary Drone, who could only see one vile day following another. To Mary, the Jubal Early Homes was a slovenly barracks entirely populated by pregnant women and new mothers whose conversation was limited to gynecology and the lack of money. Life for John Drone and his male neighbors was not nearly so onerous, for they spent their days at work in the various-hued city and returned to this barracks at night only to eat and lie with their wives—two acts which, in conjunction, make wilderness a Paradise, as the poet has pointed out. Therefore it was not John, but Mary, who went quietly mad and read the Saturday real-estate section of the *Washington Star* and concluded the only thing to do was buy a house.

"Buy a house?" John asked, shocked. "Why we can't even rent one, if there was one to rent. What are we going to use for money?"

"A veteran," Mary said, staring at the advertisements, struggling for belief, "doesn't need money. These houses are sold for nothing down if you're a veteran and can get a Veterans Administration loan guarantee."

"But we don't want a house," John pleaded. "Suppose there's something to this rumor our office will be decentralized? And we're transferred to another city? What would we do with the house then?"

"Sell it," Mary said acidly. "It isn't whether we want a house or not. Just what do you think you're going to rent? Besides," she said, reading on, "it's just like rent. You pay sixty-five dollars a month—I think we could manage that—and all the time you're paying rent, you're really saving money, because you're putting it into the house. And what do we have for our money now? Just a drawer full of old rent receipts. Anyway, where do you think we could rent a house for sixty-five dollars? Or even an apartment for sixty-five dollars?"

"But a house," John muttered. "I don't think we're ready for a house . . ."

Mary put down the paper and glared across their shabby room.

"It may surprise you to know," she said coldly, "that we are the parents of two children. I can't imagine two people any readier."

"Well," John said, "I guess it won't hurt us to look."

He pursed his lips and frowned judiciously.

"If we don't like it, we can always sell it and get another one later on," he said, completely unaware he was echoing her thought. "The way things are now, I guess we might even sell it at a profit. Where is this place?"

"Right here in Virginia," Mary said.

Only a man of vision, a real-estate promoter, say, could have seen promise in that bleak stretch of pine barrens in Fairfax County which was to be the site of Rolling Knolls Estates. (Yes, Virginia, there is a Fairfax County, but Rolling Knolls Estates is a mythical development firmly grounded, unfortunately, on the shoals of fact.)

When the Drones arrived that next Saturday in a rented car, they found bulldozers squirming over the landscape, battering down the pines, leveling the knolls, churning the area into a level red-clay sea, out of which skeletal houses were rising. A concrete entrance-drive turned off the lane-and-a-half, high-crown, macadam county highway. It stopped abruptly beside the one completed structure—a gaily-painted little house bearing the legend "Sample Home—Office." Floodlights apparently illuminated it at night.

It was quite early in the morning, but cars were parked for half a mile along the county road, and the Drones found themselves part of a slowly-moving line of young house-hunters. In a dream they inspected the tiny building, stared at the strange, yet somehow uncomfortable-looking modernistic furniture, at the picture window which seemed to make the living room so much larger. There were two small bedrooms and a little bath, and the bath was part of a central unit which on one wall was the closet, on another the "utility closet" containing the hot-water heater and oil furnace, and on the fourth wall, the kitchen range and icebox. The living room was built in the form of a shallow L, with the short leg of the L leading off the kitchen and identified as the "dining alcove." There was an attic which could be expanded into a set of bedrooms, the salesman said, and the house was solidly based on a concrete slab.

"This unique foundation," the salesman said, "does away with the need of expensive excavation. It cuts down the building cost and is one reason why all this can be offered for the amazingly low price of $10,500."

Since the house was a simple rectangle with a steep-to roof, it was basically a Cape Cod design, the salesman said, summoning up mental pictures of sun, sand, sparkling surf and sea breezes. And, because of the picture window, borrowed from California ranch homes, and because of the one-floor plan which made it easy to add another room at a later time, the house was also something of a California rambler.

"We call it the California Cape Cod Rambler," the salesman said with quiet pride.

John Drone listened and nodded sagely, while the salesman showed Mary the Formica-topped sink, the tiny kitchen that was to make housework so simple, and the dining alcove so handy to the stove.

"Everything is easy to reach, right at hand," the salesman explained.

Truer words were never spoken, for a tall woman would have been able to stand in the dining alcove, reach into the kitchen, and prepare dinner.

John and Mary looked around at the neat, clean little house and compared it to their Jubal Early apartment. There was, of course, no comparison. For one thing, the house boasted forty-eight square feet more floor space than their apartment. It did not occur to Mary until much later that the one closet in the house was even smaller than the one closet at the Jubal Early Homes, nor did it occur to John that the expansible attic was simply an air space, and therefore could appropriately be used for summer bedrooms only by deceased, unrepentant sinners. Indeed, the only question in the Drones' minds was, How soon would the other houses be built, and when could they move into one of them?

It seemed there was a waiting list. There was also the matter of John's Veterans Administration loan guarantee, and to get a certificate of eligibility for such a guarantee took a certain amount of time, for Veterans Administration had its own waiting lists. Next, John would have to obtain a Veterans Administration appraisal on the house he was to buy, and next, to discover a bank or other lending agency willing to accept a four-per-cent mortgage.

"Don't worry," the salesman said. " 'Bout the time you folks are ready to buy and move in, we'll have the house for you."

"And there's nothing down?" John asked, looking for some catch.

"Ab-so-lutely nothing," the salesman said. "Just the settlement charges. Of course," he said, "you'll have to pay for a credit check we'll make on you, and you'll have to pay the appraisal fee, and for the title search, guarantee and insurance, assume your share of the taxes, insurance on the house, and pay a few notary fees. But it shouldn't come to more than $275.76—approximately, of course."

"Oh," John said.

He didn't make that much money in a month, and they were able to save nothing, but perhaps by relentless economy, by borrowing from Mary's mother, they could scrape together the settlement fee by the time a house was ready. And so, without further reflection, John entered his name

*"We'll have the house ready for you by the time
you're ready to move in."*

on the list of prospective purchasers of one of the Rolling
Knolls Estates.

Thinking it over in the comparative sanity of his apartment that night, John Drone couldn't understand why he
was going to be charged to furnish to other people things
they required. A grocer didn't pay his customers to cart
the food out of the store, so why should a builder who wished
to check John's credit rating ask John to pay him to do so?

Why should John pay to have the title searched, when
obviously it should be up to the builder to furnish the
guarantee that title to the property was free and clear? And
why should John have to pay a staggering fee to a title

corporation to search, guarantee and insure a title which that very firm had, not two months ago, searched, guaranteed and insured for the builder?

And why should John pay the builder to have the Veterans Administration appraise the house, since logically, if the builder wished to offer the houses for sale to veterans, it would seem up to the builder to make sure he could legally do so?

Of course, there was nothing wrong with John's logic. It was simply that the building world was out of step with John, and still is.

The Rolling Knolls settlement costs were nagging, but by no means exorbitant when compared to other builders' practices. In many cases throughout the nation, builders were charging as much as $700 to $1500 for these same settlement "services." But, the Veterans Administration complained, they hid them in the mortage payments, and advertised their shoddy goods for "No Cash Down—No Down Payment, No Settlement Charges, Nothing, Nothing, Nothing Down." In fact, things reached such gaudy heights of greed that in July 1955, the Veterans Administration demanded purchasers put up a three-per-cent down payment to bring phony settlement charges back within a more normal range of legal larceny.

John Drone's major difficulty, however, was finding a bank willing to accept what bankers were already calling "GI paper." Since John had never been in debt in his life, and had no charge accounts, and had always paid spot cash for his modest purchases, it turned out—to his utter amazement —that his credit rating was zero.

"But," he asked in perplexity, "why shouldn't it be the best there is, because I've never been in debt?"

"Your credit rating," a prim office girl told him, "is based on your ability to repay your debts."

"You mean, if I haven't been able to pay for something, say a pair of stockings, except in dribs and drabs, that makes my credit rating better than if I'd been able to pay cash for the stockings?"

"Exactly," she said.

"I see," said John, who didn't.

In time, however, John was to see the financial world's point of view perfectly well. He was to arrive at a point in life where he owed money for everything he ate, drank, wore and used, and then, naturally, his credit rating became A-1.

Because of his lack of credit rating, however, and because every Washington banker with whom he talked couldn't have been less interested in a four-per-cent mortgage when there was an even brisker business in non-GI mortgages bearing five and six per cent, John found himself taking his troubles again to the builder, the Samuel O. Burmal Realty Co., Inc.

"Think nothing of it," the office girl told him. "The SOB Suburban Bank and Trust and Home Loan Agency will be glad to handle it."

She smiled a bright, fiscal smile and uttered a little speech.

"Mr. Burmal knows you veterans are the finest young men in America," she said rapidly, "and your word is our bond. Mr. Burmal says anybody who could lick Hitler could pay his bills, if he has a steady job."

She glanced at John's credit check.

"And you have a *government* job," she said. "All we require is your signature and your certificate of eligibility. Mr. Burmal is able to do this, because he has faith in you, and because he has faith in himself. Rolling Knolls is really a Samuel O. Burmal production from start to finish."

She smiled her mechanical smile again and pushed a document across the glass-topped desk.

"Sign here," she said.

In signing, John Drone imagined he was completing another step toward the purchase of a $10,500 house. He never once considered he was going to buy a $10,500 "house and lot." There was a subtle difference here, one completely understood by Samuel O. Burmal, who had first foreseen the possibilities inherent in ninety acres of pine barrens not six miles from Washington. He'd bought the land before the war had ended, and by the time the first veterans were streaming home, he'd completed his arrangements.

First, Mr. Burmal formed a number of Delaware corporations. As the SOB Investment Co., Inc., he bought the land at $300 an acre. He promptly sold it to the SOB Land Co., Inc., for $600 an acre, accepting a commission en route for SOB Investment to reduce taxes.

THEREUPON:

SOB Land sold the property for $1200 an acre to SOB Promotions, again extracting a commission. SOB Promotions promptly unloaded the property to a customer—SOB Realty —for $2400 an acre, and Mr. Burmal, as the realty company, promised SOB Promotions to improve the land by streets, sewers and an electric power line.

WHEREUPON:

SOB Realty chopped eighty-three of the acres into six generous lots per acre—for Mr. Burmal was not the kind of greedy operator who sold one-eighth-acre lots—and offered each lot for sale at $3000. Thus, before work of any kind began, Mr. Burmal could thoughtfully consider his $24,900

First, he formed a number of Delaware corporations.

investment in building acreage had already acquired a $1,494,000 potential—a paper profit of $1,469,100.

All along the way, Mr. Burmal had sold himself the land under release clauses, whereby neither title nor cash were to be exchanged, except for nominal down payments to himself, until the final sale to the ultimate veteran. The only cost Mr. Burmal would someday have to face on his successive 100-per-cent profits would be the tax on the profit of each land sale. But, by dragging things out over six-month intervals, Mr. Burmal's corporations were able to pay only capital gains taxes.

In all this, Mr. Burmal was merely repeating the ageless pattern of subdivision promotions, which primarily depend on kited land values. Mr. Burmal was doing nothing precisely illegal, although spoilsports might suggest there was a certain aura of nepotism about the amicable business relationships his corporations enjoyed. At any rate, Mr. Burmal had been in the business for some years, and at a prior time had acquired the SOB Suburban Bank & Trust and Home Loan Agency. It was perhaps inevitable that Mr. Burmal applied to this bank for a building loan.

The bank knew a bargain when it saw one. It, too, had faith in Mr. Burmal, the veteran's friend. The bank knew the Federal Government, through Veterans Administration guarantees, would back nearly two thirds of the amount it would cost to build each house. Further, the bank knew the houses would sell in a flash, and thus the bank saw fit to use its depositors' money and its own investments to guarantee 80 per cent of the mortgage sums. On houses and lots to be sold for $10,500 each, this came to $8400 per house and lot.

Thus, Mr. Burmal, now ready to build his 498 houses,

knew where to get $4,183,200 with which to do so. Naturally, all this money was not forthcoming at one time—the bank's payments to the actual constructing engineer, SOB Construction, Inc., would be spaced out over a considerable period.

Now, dear hearts, if Mr. Burmal was to sell each lot for $3000, it meant the house would have to cost $7500. As the contractor, Mr. Burmal permitted himself the not-excessive-by-current-standard profit of 15 per cent per house. And so, what with the $900 difference between the mortgage guarantee and the house sales price, and the $1065 profit per house to the builder, Mr. Burmal moodily contemplated a $1965 profit per house before the first nail was driven. Since there were to be 498 houses built, he anticipated a little windfall of $976,770 right off the bat. Eventually, of course, there'd be time to estimate the twenty years of interest at four per cent on $5,229,000 worth of mortgages.

Mr. Burmal regretted, but could not avoid, the fact that he'd have to gerrymander the extra seven acres of his original land purchase into streets, and to install these and sewers and electric lines at a cost of some $750,000. But he accepted this as philosophically as he accepted the fact that he'd have to pay taxes and commissions and salaries to his office staff and carpenters, and to deduct the cost of his original investment. But, after all, he was starting a $5,229,-000 subdivision on $27,000, and the two pencils he wore out doing his arithmetic—chiefly addition—could be regarded as a tax loss.

In fact, being a cautious man and getting on in years, Mr. Burmal was quite willing to discount the entire five-million-dollar mortgage to a couple of hayseed banks in the hinterlands for as much as twenty per cent, dissolve all his corporations, sell his bank, get out from under everything, and retire to Babylonian luxury in Miami as soon as the last house in Rolling Knolls Estates was sold. And he knew, for he was a man of vision, that it wouldn't take long.

Still, it occurred to Mr. Burmal there might be another dollar or two to be found in Rolling Knolls before he left. Mr. Burmal had submitted his plans to the government—which would allot him priorities on building materials for veterans' housing—on a one-house-cost basis. If he were to build the houses all alike, in mass production, he could shave actual construction costs at a further profit. If he found a friendly appraiser, his brother-in-law Roger Cutpurse, for instance, he might be permitted to pour each concrete walkway a few inches too narrow; he might be able to put the rafters a mite farther apart and so save maybe 1000 rafters. You know, things like that. It's the little things that count, and Mr. Burmal was ever aware that a penny saved is a penny earned.

Now John Drone, of course, was aware of none of the various processes of Mr. Burmal's mind any more than he was aware of the manner in which the Veterans Administration was to regard its guarantee of veterans' mortgages. All John knew, in his own vague way, was that he'd have to pay several thousand dollars in interest over and above the value of what he thought was a "$10,500 house." Since this interest stretched over twenty years, and could be regarded as rent, John took refuge in the quaint notion he could meanwhile create an equity in his property—save money, really—so that at the end of his mortgage term, he'd have increased his present worth by $10,500.

It never occurred to him that for nearly half the mortgage term he'd be paying practically pure interest and creating very little equity, nor did he stop to think that in twenty years a house and lot such as his might not bring ten cents at a spirited public auction.

Even less did it occur to John Drone he was buying a house and lot that would have cost him $6485 if he'd bought the land and had hired carpenters to nail the shack together, for he could never have raised that sum. Thus, Drone was in effect paying Mr. Burmal a premium of $4015 for Mr. Burmal's services, not to mention paying Mr. Burmal twenty years' worth of four-per-cent interest on $10,500 as well.

Mary Drone's thoughts were much less complex. From the beginning, she'd looked upon the house as an expedient—indeed as the only expedient—but for the conscious moment, the estate at Rolling Knolls seemed to her a combination of nirvana and the Promised Land.

"It has light and space and will be our very own," Mary said, deep in a private female dream.

"And after a while, we'll be able to save money," John said. "I won't always be making fifty dollars a week."

When settlement day came, the Drones again rented a car and drove to Rolling Knolls. The county's high-crown road was now lumpy and pitted from an unaccustomed load of construction vehicles but remained as narrow as ever, and where there had been one bright sample house rising bravely from a sea of mud, there were now hundreds of houses, just as neat and small as the sampler. Squads and platoons of these little boxes marched in close order beside what seemed to be red-clay canals. Each house was surrounded by a patch of bilious sod, and two rusty dwarf cedars struggled for life beside each identical doorstep. They were the only trees in all Rolling Knolls.

"Yessir," the salesman said, clapping John on the back,

"completely landscaped. Streets will be in any day now. But I know you folks are pretty anxious to move right in, aren't you?

"Well," he said, shuffling the papers on his desk, "it's all ready for you—Number Thirteen, Bataan Boulevard. It was Mr. Burmal's idea," he confided, "to name the streets after the battles you kids won for us old stay-at-homes. Wish I could have gone, but they wouldn't have me. Well, anyway. . ."

"Could we see it before we sign the papers?" Mary wanted to know.

"Sure thing," the salesman said. "I have the keys right here."

He stepped toward the door and paused.

"Tell you what," he said, "the streets are pretty muddy today and your house is down at the end of this street, Salerno Avenue, then left down Iwo Jima one block, and then right on Bataan, and yours is the house on the next corner."

"Oh, good," Mary said, "a corner house."

"Yes, you're one of the lucky ones," the salesman chuckled.

As a matter of fact, the Drones *were* lucky in their corner lot, for it is to Mr. Burmal's credit—or possibly due to a strange oversight—that there was no extra charge for corner lots in Rolling Knolls. The subdivision had been laid out in a grid, but in a near-by development, and in countless developments across the face of the nation, things were not so rectilinear. The development adjacent to Rolling Knolls had curving streets with little circular cul-de-sacs leading off the streets. The lots around the cul-de-sacs were pie-shaped, and were therefore called "corner lots." In that subdivision, a corner lot cost $250 more, and, until imitators appeared, that subdivision was the only one in the whole wide world with nine "corner lots" on each "corner."

"We could go down there now, if you wish," the salesman was saying, "but like I say, it's kind of muddy today. Anyway, it's just like this house. They're all alike. And your contract says your house is just like this one, so you're really not buying sight unseen."

"Oh, no," John agreed, "we're not." He permitted himself a tight-lipped little smirk, intended to show the salesman that he, John Drone, was no fool.

An office girl entered the room, identified herself as a notary, and very shortly John and Mary affixed their signatures to a document committing them to pay sixty-five dollars a month every month for the next twenty years, in return for which they would be allowed to live in a house "like" the sample house for every month they continued to pay the sixty-five dollars. In short, they bought a "home of their own," sight more or less seen.

As they left the office, the house keys in John's pocket, Mary couldn't resist temptation, mud or no. And mud it would have to be, for all the lots bore signs, "New Sod, Keep Off." John took a tentative step off the pavement in front of the sample house and promptly sank into liquid red clay over his shoe-top.

"Let's take off our shoes and socks," Mary said, delighted and irresponsible as the child she'd been when she'd married John on furlough during the war. "We'll leave them here, and you carry Chip and I'll carry the baby."

Off they trudged down the squelchy road, down Salerno to Iwo Jima to Bataan, ankle-deep in mud, carrying their children, two refugees of the postwar years.

The key turned stiffly in the lock, and John had to throw

his weight three times against the already-warped door before it burst open and he half sprawled into his new living room.

"Door's a little stiff yet," he muttered.

They tracked red clay across the parquet floor and inspected the rooms still smelling of new paint. Carpenters had left their traces, as carpenters will—little bits of wood and shavings, an occasional bent nail or two, three empty paint cans and the crust of a lunchtime sandwich. Through their picture window, a vast and empty eye with bits of paper stuck in its corners, they could see their view—a house like theirs across a muddy street, its vacant picture eye staring into theirs.

Mary all at once had that eerie sensation everyone has at one time or another—that somehow she'd lived this identical moment in the past. She groped in the attic of her mind for some memory of a place, of a name, that would provide a clue to the reason for her sudden presentiment. It was perhaps just as well for her that she did not think of the Jubal Early Homes.

2. An' the Walls Come Tumblin' Down

THERE WAS a brisk staccato on Mary Drone's warped front door, and on the stoop Mary encountered a stringy woman in tweeds; a woman who transfixed Mary with a glittering eye and whose small talk was a gust of rifle fire.

"I'd like to know what you're going to do about these streets," she told Mary. "I'm Mrs. H. Ardis Voter I live on Iwo Jima these streets are a disgrace and we're not going to let them get away with it we're forming a citizens' association come to our workshop at eight Wednesday evening at my house, sixty-four Iwo Jima bring your husband I can see from here your plaster's cracked, too, may I come in?"

Mary mumbled, "Of course," and hopped aside as Mrs. Voter strode manfully into the living room.

"Mygod," Mrs. Voter said, "your floor is all waves, too. What else do you have besides the street, the cracked plaster and the floors? How are your walls, how thick is your slab?"

"My husband said the floor would settle," Mary began. "He said all new houses settle a bit, and the salesman came and said all parquet flooring has to settle into place. But frankly, I think it has already settled . . . like that."

She gestured helplessly.

"Well," Mrs. Voter said complacently, "we're not going to let them get away with this but nobody can do anything all by himself what we need is integrated community action that's why we're forming a citizens' association."

And thus it was the Drones first met their new neighbors, making friendships under much the same auspices as friendships are hastily formed in the pitching lifeboat, pulling away from the sinking steamer across a wild night sea. For such is the way all first friendships are formed in any new postwar suburban development.

In the Voters' house they met the Faints, the Amiables, the Fecunds and the Wilds. They also met the Spleens, whose attitude was cold, and who—although the Drones were never aware of it—were already the Drones' mortal enemies. It seems the movers had tracked a path across the Spleens' new sod to carry the Drones' chattels into the Drones' new manor, and Mrs. Spleen, peering out through the venetian blinds of her picture window, had given a telephonic blow-by-blow account of the affair to her apoplectic husband in his Washington office. And the Drones met Mr. Voter, a black-haired, dynamic little lawyer for the Office of Price Administration's Bureau of Contradictory Regulations; a man who talked knowingly in terms of civil suit. Out of this meeting came the Rolling Knolls Citizens' Association, conceived in fury and dedicated to revenge. It was agreed to send a petition to the Veterans Administration, and Mrs. Voter was unanimously elected chairwoman.

At roughly the same time, similar meetings of disillusioned young home-buyers were under way across the face of the

North American continent. In the nine months between July 1, 1947, and March 1948, the Housing Expediter's office in Washington received 31,233 veterans' complaints against builders. The plain fact was, the chisel was the tool most often used to construct the postwar development house, and the chisel's popularity with builders has not decreased with the passing years. It is one of the touching love affairs of all time.

As early as 1948, the Agriculture Department's pathologists reported decay organisms flourishing beneath 85 per cent of houses inspected on behalf of the Housing and Home Finance Agency. Ill-vented crawl spaces trapped moist, humid air, and in this fetid jungle atmosphere underpinnings rotted, structural decay set in at once, and floors sagged dangerously.

. . . pathologists reported decay organisms flourishing . . .

In 1952, a House Select Committee, under Representative Olin Teague of Texas, made a sweeping investigation of housing built under the GI Bill in twenty-six cities. The committee found everywhere indications of the skillfully-wielded chisel. Veteran purchasers complained of no insulation, of missing streets, sidewalks and driveways—sometimes of missing rooms. Linoleum had been substituted for tile in bathrooms, refrigerators were missing, as were window and door screens, waterproofing and weatherstripping; one coat of paint had been applied instead of three; floors were knotty, splintery horrors; lawns eroded due to slipshod grading and sodding; tin or lead served instead of the paid-for copper flashing and pipes; pine took the place of oak, plywood took the place of pine, there was bad wiring; concrete slabs were poured two inches thick instead of twelve; tops and bottoms of doors were unsealed, unpainted; and in one subdivision refrigerators were so placed that their doors could not be opened.

In Baltimore a builder had managed, by shaving a foot off the dimensions of each of some sixty houses, to put up ninety-four houses on a tract zoned for ninety. In Billings, Montana, a veteran found morning-glories bursting into his living room through the crack appearing between the sinking concrete slab and the baseboards of the walls. In Corpus Christi, Texas, one householder discovered his bathtub not connected with the sewer pipes—the water simply poured into the crawl space below his bedroom. In Bednar Lake, Oklahoma, houses built on an old lake bed were flooded with an inch of red mud. In Philadelphia, a veteran's radiant-heating went blooie, and he had to rip up his concrete slab with a jackhammer, hunting the defective pipes. He finally found them, not in the slab, but laid under it on the ground —and the pipes were iron, not copper.

The Teague committee sifted this noxious salmagundi and found evidence of "widespread criminal conspiracy" on the part of Veterans Administration loan guaranty officials, fee appraisers and inspectors, officials of lending institutions and builders. Indictments were turned in by juries in Miami, San Diego, Providence, Rhode Island; Wilmington, Delaware; Detroit, Lubbock, Texas; Oklahoma City, Los Angeles and San Antonio. The crimes consisted of bribery, lies and evasions of building laws and regulations. By 1950, veterans had collected $2,262,545 in compensatory damages from builders, but this was a drop in the bucket, for the Teague committee reported that veterans in the Washington metropolitan area—where the Drones lived—were bilked of "millions of dollars" by unscrupulous builders. And, lest this be thought a thing of the past, on February 29, 1956, Thomas J. Sweeney, chief of Veterans Administration's loan guaranty office, was reported as telling an American Legion audience the government has "failed miserably" in its responsibilities and that veterans were still being gypped, and that Veterans Administration construction inspectors—fee appraisers—were still being fired.

While some veteran-purchasers got a little of their own back from builders, such was not the case in Rolling Knolls. Mrs. Voter, her muddy features ashen, read the Veterans Administration's reply to the assembled Citizens' Association. It had arrived that very morning, St. Valentine's Day. The gist of it was, the Veterans Administration guaranteed only the loan; not the construction of the house. VA would not and could not, the note said, take each veteran by the hand and wipe his nose for him. If a man buys a house, the curt note said, it is always a case of buyer beware, and the Veterans Administration did not conceive that its duties included running a free course for veterans on how to buy a house. Veterans Administration was satisfied, the note said, if the appraiser's evaluation coincided with the sales price. As a kind of sop to everyone's sensibilities, the note admitted the Veterans Administration often granted loan guarantees on houses that did not measure up to the Federal Housing Administration's standards.

"But they can't say this," Mrs. Voter nearly wailed. "The house itself is part of the security for the loan. They can't refuse to protect their own investments, made with the taxpayers' money."

But they could. And did. And still do. The Rolling Knolls Citizens' Association petition had been addressed to a dead-letter office.

It was just as the Teague committee was later to report on the metropolitan Washington scene, that Veterans Administration conceived the loan guaranty program "to be a builder's program, rather than a veterans' program, and operated on the assumption that the builder must be pacified at all costs, without regard to the effect . . . on the home-owner veteran."

All of which left the good burghers of Rolling Knolls with just one place to go—to Mr. Burmal's office. But here they had a jolly surprise, for Mr. Burmal's office came to them. It came in the form of Franklin Galahad, supervising engineer of SOB Construction, Inc., accompanied by Roger Cutpurse, Mr. Burmal's brother-in-law, commissioned by the Veterans Administration as fee appraiser for the Rolling Knolls development. The two men called together at each house in turn.

"Whatsa matta ya don't like ya house?" Mr. Galahad demanded. "Roger—Mr. Cutpurse here—OK'd the appraisal, didn't he?"

"Our place isn't like the sample house at all," John Drone

began, reeling from Mr. Galahad's direct attack, grasping frantically for bits and pieces of Mr. and Mrs. Voter's advice. "Our floor's warped and the door won't shut, and it's made out of pine instead of oak, and the streets. . ."

"OK, OK, OK," Mr. Galahad said, holding up a giant hand. "Let's calm down. Let's take it easy. Let's take it one at a time. Now, for instance, ya gotta house like the sample house. Of course, ya didn't getta house exactly like the sample house, but where in ya contract does it say ya should? Nowhere, is where. If it said in the contract an exact facsimile, that's something else again. But it don't say that inna contract. Ya read ya contract, bub?"

Ah, the contract. As a matter of fact, John Drone had never read that contract all the way through, and what he'd read of it didn't mean much to him one way or another. The fact was, that contract didn't mean much at all, as we'll see.

"If ya go down to VA," Mr. Galahad said heavily, "ya'll see the plans for ya house. They're on file. Ya'll see we followed them plans right down to the last nail. We also got the plans for the sample house on file there, too. When we built the sample house, we followed *them* plans. What I say is, ya house is like the sample house, but not *just* like it, see? They really got two different plans. If ya'd ordered the sample house it woulda cost ya $750 more, see?"

Dimly, John Drone saw. It seemed reasonable to him, put in these terms, that perhaps his judgment of Mr. Burmal's building had been too hasty.

"So the floor does warp a little," Mr. Galahad was saying, his voice now an oleaginous flood. "The wood we gotta use today—honest, whaddya expect? All parquet flooring warps some, don't it, Roger?"

"Mr. Burmal would like to, but he can't," Mr. Galahad explained.

"Can't help that," Mr. Cutpurse agreed heartily. "Sure does."

"Well, what about the streets?" Mary Drone burst out, seeing her husband wavering. "How long is this mud going to be tracked into my house?"

"Ya can't put the streets in now—gotta wait for the weather," Mr. Galahad said. "When the weather settles down, ya can put them in."

"What do you mean, 'you'? You mean you, or we?" John Drone asked, filled with a sudden panic.

"Well, listen," Mr. Galahad said soothingly, "we're not going to be able to do it. Mr. Burmal would like to, but he can't. Mr. Burmal wanted to put streets in, but gee, if he did, where'd be the profit? But you people can put 'em in—or, if ya get together like ya do, and ask the county, the county'll put 'em right in. Soon as the weather breaks, of course. I am right, Roger?"

"County would be glad to," Mr. Cutpurse said promptly. "On an assessment basis."

"You told us—your salesman told us—the streets would be in 'any day now,' didn't he, Mary?" John said, feeling the ground give way. "He told us you'd put the streets in."

"An' where in ya contract does it say streets?" Mr. Galahad demanded coldly. "Look in ya contract. It says there any agreement not made a part of the contract is not binding on the seller. Doesn't it? Sure, it does. Ya don't expect us to put in the contract everything that comes into some salesman's head, do ya? Some of them guys would offer ya the moon to get a commission."

Mr. Galahad shook his heavy head in wonderment at the things salesmen will sometimes say.

"But we're in business," he continued briskly. "Whyncha read the contract over before ya sent in that petition?"

"You mean we're—you're not going to build the streets you promised?" Mary wanted to know.

"Look, lady," Mr. Galahad said humbly, "Mr. Burmal wanted to put in them streets. He wanted them called after him—ya know—Burmal Roads. . ."

"That's what we call them now," John snapped.

". . . But like I tell ya, he just can't," Mr. Galahad explained. "Can he Roger?"

"No," Mr. Cutpurse said.

"Now that petition," Mr. Galahad said. "That really hurt Mr. Burmal, to hear people saying things like that. Especially, because do ya remember the day ya signed the contract? When it came closing day," he continued, "ya signed two supplemental forms that were made part of the contract. One said ya agreed to waive 'any and all defects or deviations of every kind and character,' an' 'released the seller from any claims, now or hereafter.' Remember that? An' the other form ya signed said ya agreed never to go to no government agency of no kind, FHA, VA, or nobody, to complain, but to come to the builder if ya had any trouble. Remember that?"

"We came to see you," Mr. Cutpurse said smoothly, "because my brother-in-law, Mr. Burmal, thought it was all a mistake. He felt someone in Rolling Knolls, someone with some imagined grudge, just got everybody stampeded into forgetting what was in the contract. So we came to have this little personal chat."

"An' that's what I call white of him," Mr. Galahad said. "Anybody else but Sam Burmal . . . gee, anybody else might of just sued ya for breach of contract on a thing like that."

"Is there anything else we can do for you folks?" Mr. Cutpurse asked.

"I guess not, thanks," John said. And Mr. Galahad and

Mr. Cutpurse walked across the eroded lawn to see the Spleens.

Once again, it must not be imagined the Drones and their fellow passengers in the storm-tossed lifeboat were alone in their agony.

"The majority of sales contracts used in the sale of new homes to veteran purchasers are inadequate," the Teague committee reported. "In many instances, contracts are inadequate in details relating to responsibility for streets, sidewalks and sewers. These contracts afford little or no protection to the veteran purchaser. Plans and specifications are not incorporated into the contract; data relating to specific closing costs is inadequate; a definite performance date is not specified; most contracts do not contain guaranties or warranties on heating, plumbing and electrical fixtures, or guaranty for a dry basement, or for a satisfactory septic tank and sound roof."

In many cases in the Drones' Washington area, the report said, the contract "is so indefinite that it actually fails to indicate the veteran will receive a house."

The committee said such supplemental forms as the Drones signed on settlement day were merely attempts of the builder to "abridge or invalidate" the already sketchy contract itself.

And why had the Drones and their neighbors signed such ridiculous contracts? The answer is twofold. First, few young veterans had any business experience, and practically none had experience in real-estate ventures. Second, John Drone and his friends, in their desperate need for living space, pushed into places like Rolling Knolls because no other quarters were available on their market, would have signed any contract put in front of them. These facts were duly noted by such operators as Mr. Burmal, whose contract forms were studies in arrogance and contempt.

There is absolutely no reason to believe that things have improved in this field of human relations in the last four years. Unfortunately, there'll always be a contract, and since the same builders are building the same houses in the same way, the chances are excellent that the contracts have changed no more than any other feature of the modern sub-division. If you, like the Drones, live in a development, or are thinking of moving to a development, curiosity should lead you to read your contract. Just for fun, see if it mentions a house.

Jane and Henry Amiable had been just as shocked as John and Mary Drone and the Voters to find the appraiser was Mr. Burmal's brother-in-law. What the Spleens thought of the matter couldn't be sent through the mails, and on those grounds will be omitted here, despite the fact it was a general view. The consensus of the subsequent Thursday night meeting of the Rolling Knolls Citizens' Association was that the whole affair seemed a trifle gamey. But once again, there was nothing to be done about it.

The Teague committee complained that appraisers were not civil servants, but were private fee-appraisers authorized by Veterans Administration to peek at houses offered for sale on the GI plan. In the Washington area, where the Drones lived, there was no evidence of criminal conspiracy, but "incompetence on the part of loan guaranty officials and favoritism toward certain builders, real-estate brokers and compliance inspectors [appraisers]. The compliance inspection system has been virtually ineffective. . ."

Thus, in the Washington area, certain appraisers, Roger Cutpurse among them, waxed fat while others waxed lean.

Or, as the Teague committee pointed out, "the bulk of appraisal fees went out to a favored few," with the result that one appraiser received $57,573 in fees on GI-loan houses he inspected for Veterans Administration over a four-year period, while another, perhaps not so gregarious a person, received only $13,546 in inspection fees for Veterans Administration over the same period.

In all this, the rule was that the appraiser who allowed the builder an optimistic estimate of the building's worth was more in demand among the builders who hired the appraisers than some killjoy whose appraisal was, shall we say, more realistic.

In more venal communities, however, the story was slightly different. In Detroit, for example, it was discovered appraisers came cheap. A builder purchased one there for five bottles of whisky, a basket of fruit, a chafing dish full of nuts, four turkeys, two hams, a carving set, a punchbowl full of Christmas goodies, a fruitcake, linen, and ninety-five dollars' worth of gift certificates. Compared to the outlay in this case, the builder had the giddy experience of casting crumbs upon the waters, to find that they came back in the form of several thousand sandwiches.

Taking things all in all, the Teague committee suggested appraisers should be made civil servants; that they should be prevented by law from taking gifts from builders; that the whole Veterans Administration loan guaranty division should be overhauled; that the veteran-purchaser should be given a book warning him of the pitfalls of home-buying, and—getting to the heart of things—that builders should be required to put up cash warranties against defects and frauds. Oddly enough, this last aspect of the Teague committee's report was considered unrealistic by the Veterans Administration and—of all people—by the National Association of Home Builders.

The Veterans Administration spokesmen argued that they were interested only in getting homes built for veterans. Nothing should stand in the way of this great civic need. If builders were badgered by a superfluity of regulations, the builders might not build, and what would the poor veteran do then?

This was precisely the point of the National Association of Home Builders, who also pointed out it was only the most despicable of their number who were frauds, fly-by-nights, and cheap-Jacks. Reputable builders, the association said, had nothing to do with such people, and therefore there was no need of applying stringent limitations (such as putting up warranties) to reputable men whose word was very nearly their bond. Any further limitation on the building trades, the association's spokesmen intoned, might have the result of fewer houses for veterans.

All this left the Teague committee muttering that the government ought to take some steps to protect itself when it guaranteed a loan of the taxpayers' money, but the committee was mumbling in a wilderness. Or, as the *New York Times* reported, "leaders of the home building industry fought bitterly, and successfully, against the warranty provisions." Building proceeded apace.

There seemed to the Rolling Knolls Citizens' Association no place to turn for help with their many problems now that Mr. Burmal and the United States Government had failed them. But Mrs. Voter suggested banging on the doors of the county and, ultimately, of the state government. At once the new citizens of Rolling Knolls discovered problems that made them forget the seamier aspects of their sticking doors and rippling floors. They ran at once into a new American situation—again one in which hundreds of thousands of suburban-development householders all across the nation were to find themselves.

Mrs. Voter's delegation was received with something less than marked enthusiasm by the established county machine government, which might have appeared to a heartless soul to have been dozing in the sun on the courthouse steps for a hundred years before Appomattox.

This was the county government which, to all intents and purposes, seemed to function as a zoning board only at a distant country crossroads at midnight, to plot the erection of a rendering plant in a residential neighborhood. If this sounds unfair, consider: Usually only the builders appeared before the meetings of the county zoning board, because the builders alone had advance notice of the meetings—since they had requested them—and only the builders had had time to prepare their plans and stuff their briefcases, while the householders in the area were innocent of their schemes, or, at the last minute, when they heard of the meeting, could not escape their daily offices or their household chores. Wherever the fault lies, the fact is this: Neither of the two northern Virginia counties adjacent to the city of Washington shows the slightest evidence of any attention paid to zoning problems, and for proof of this matter, one has only to visit them. As far as civic planning is concerned, both Arlington and Fairfax counties resemble a dog's breakfast.

The county officials were pleased to meet with Mrs. Ardis Voter's friends of Rolling Knolls, but for a reason Mrs. Voter least suspected. The county's folksy fathers saw in Rolling Knolls and kindred subdivisions a vast new tax base. Perhaps now there would be money to build those roads the rump-

*The builders alone had advance notice of
the meeting of the zoning board.*

sprung, down-county farmers had wanted for so many years. Maybe they could afford at last to put up that long-planned statue to General Robert E. Lee.

So Mrs. Voter told the Southern gentlemen the sad story of the no streets at Rolling Knolls, and demanded (for she was a demanding person) to know what the county was going to do about building schools for all the sudden new youngsters. The county governors heard her politely and, after she'd left, happily figured out the new assessment base. They weren't too much interested in Rolling Knolls per se. After all, the place was filled with a lot of damnyankee foreigners whose only saving grace was that they did have money, and those down-county white trash could have their roads and it wouldn't lose a single farmer's vote to build them.

Rolling Knolls didn't know it, but bitter political battles lay in the years ahead, all of them costly. Mrs. Voter, as principal delegate, was to spend many a day at county board meetings, and many a day more at the state assemblies in Richmond, and wherever she went, with whatever problems, she was met by the rustic belches and wheezy snores of Virginia's woodenheaded legislators. Politically, therefore, Rolling Knolls remained in that storm-tossed lifeboat, wandering about over the hideous depths of apathy, watching the feeble rockets vanish in the murk of sullen hostility.

Meanwhile, the jerry-built houses fell apart and John and Mary Drone's life sank into the suspended animation of development life, and they were not consoled by the fact they'd signed a long-term contract for the trip to oblivion.

Indeed, the only light glimmering faintly in the surrounding darkness was that will-o'-the-wisp, Do-It-Yourself. But this was not only a dancing illusion; it was a Welsh wrecker's lamp, as we shall see.

3. Life Faces Mary

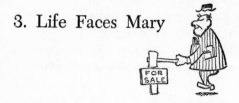

"Remember, when we talk of developments, we're really talking about women."—Harold Mendelsohn, American University

MARY DRONE'S WASHING MACHINE jittered to a stop, and as she lifted the lid to peel the wet wash from the inner walls of the contraption, year-old Kim burst into a desperate keening.

"Oh, God, what now?" Mary muttered, colliding with the opened door of an under-the-sink cabinet as she barged out of the tiny kitchen on her way to the dinette and the living room to the source of the wails.

She found Kim shrieking beside the open door of the utility closet—the space containing the hot-water heater and furnace. Kim, holding one red hand in the other, her eyes tight shut, seemed to be drawing a giant breath. Then she let it go, splitting the shattered air anew.

"She crying," Chip observed.

"Did you touch that hot-water pipe again?" Mary demanded, torn between tears and anger. She lifted the howling child to her shoulder, noticing as she did that it was time to change Kim's diaper.

The front door banged open.

"Yoo hoo! It's me!" Gladys Fecund called, hopping into the room. Then, seeing the maternal tableau, she asked with gay concern:

"Oh, dear, what's the matter now?" She patted Kim's tiny back. "Do oo hurt its 'ittle self?" she asked.

"She burned her hand on the hot-water pipe," Mary said. "I don't know why they didn't put insulation around those pipes."

"Do you want me to get some olive oil for it? Olive oil is wonderful for burns."

Mary, who as a matter of fact had been about to get a salve from the bathroom shelves, bit her lip and told Gladys never mind, it wasn't much of a burn. She just wasn't going to let another woman tell her how to care for a child. Mary put Kim down, went to the children's bedroom for a new diaper, and returned to find Gladys at the door again, ushering in her four children.

"It's not a bit nice out—for them to play," Gladys said. "It's going to rain. It's raining a little now.

"I really can't stay a minute," she said, pushing yesterday's papers off the couch to sit down. "Maybe just until the rain stops."

"Let me heat up the coffee," Mary said wearily, diaper pins in her mouth. "I'll be through in a sec."

She finished with Kim, stepped around the Fecund children squirming on the floor, and was well on her way to the kitchen when Chip's husky four-year-old cries of wounded rage beat at her ears.

"Gimmie! Mine!" her son was bellowing.

"Give it back, Jackson," Gladys was saying. "It's not yours. It's Chip's tricycle. . ."

Three hours later, 1:15 P.M., Gladys' minute was up and

she packed off her brood and decamped. Mary hadn't the faintest idea what they'd discussed, since most of the conversation had necessarily been conducted in fits and starts, coming spasmodically through a thick field of children's static. Vaguely, Mary decided the morning's chat had increased her sum of knowledge to this extent: that three persons unknown to her, but known to Gladys, had their names down on waiting lists for new cars; that Mrs. Voter thought she was going to have a baby but the doctor didn't think so. Meanwhile, it was raining.

Mary moodily gathered up the coffee cups and the saucers with their ground-out cigaret butts, and piled the debris in the littered sink. She hadn't done the breakfast dishes because she'd picked up the children's room and had sorted the wash first thing after John left on his mile-long walk to the bus stop. She saw the washing machine lid open, started to close it from force of habit, and realized she hadn't taken the wash out to dry. Chip was making Kim cry in the living room, but Mary was beyond the point of caring much about it one way or another. The beds were unmade. Gladys' kids had scattered Chip's and Kim's toys all over the house. Mary sat on the high kitchen stool and, while waiting to wonder where to begin, lit a cigaret and watched the rain fall softly over Rolling Knolls. It gathered in little pools, and gullies formed, and the gullies became tiny canyons, winding through the sparse sod.

And then it was 1:30. Mary came out of her trance with a start. In three and a half hours, John would be home. She started to extract the wash from the machine, but remembered it was time for lunch. She fixed lunch for herself and the children, piled the dishes in the sink, put the children down for their naps, made the beds, put the papers back on the couch, returned to the kitchen and did all the dishes. It was still raining. It gave every promise of raining all day and all night, and Mary knew she wouldn't hang the wash outside. Once again, she'd have to string it wetly through the house.

Gloomily, she ran the first two clotheslines across the living room, fastening them to the nails John had driven in the walls for the purpose.

Adam Wild was buying his wife a dryer.

John should buy her a dryer. They could put it—well, they couldn't put it in the kitchen. There wasn't room to turn around there, as it was. And certainly they couldn't put it in the living room; it would never fit beside the couch. Likewise, there wasn't space enough to put it in the dinette or in the bathroom, or in the children's room unless they bought the kids a two-deck bunk bed and got rid of the two sections of that old studio couch. So the dryer would have to go in what Mary called the master bedroom—just as it had in the Wilds' house. But, she thought, they wouldn't need it long—just until Kim was out of diapers, really. Then, she thought gaily, they could sell it!

The possibility of a little windfall cheered her immensely. Why money from the sale of the dryer could buy them. . .

A scalding, numbing pain shot through her right leg. Moving down the clothesline, intent on her work, she'd barked her shin against Chip's tricycle. It hurt like sin, and the tears came automatically. It was at this point the door shuddered open, and a wet wind blew in.

"Watch out, can't you see the wash is up? You're getting the wash all dirty," Mary very nearly screamed.

"I'm sorry dear," a familiar, monotonous voice said.

"Oh, it's you," Mary said.

And it was. John Drone, master of all he surveyed, had returned to his castle and to the bosom of his admiring family. He closed the door.

"Hi," he said brightly over the clothesline. "What's for chow?"

Now certainly it was not just John Drone's bumping into the wash that led Mary to shriek at him as he returned from his day at the office. The cumulative effect of Mary's rancid day led her to shriek, and although she never once allowed the thought conscious expression, somewhere deep inside her she knew perfectly well that the house she inhabited had helped spoil her day; that it was harming her marriage and corroding her life. In fact, the corrosive process was well under way, for the Drones had lived in their new rambler for six months. The pattern of their lives was bearing out the truth in Winston Churchill's dictum: "We shape our dwellings, and then our dwellings shape us."

The shape of Mary's dwelling was vile. Consider:

If there had been a basement, Mary would not have hung the wash in the living room. Hanging the wash in the living room is depressing enough, but the spectacle presented after the wash is hung is even more depressing. The soul, contemplative at day's end, does not soar through a curtain of soggy shirts.

Had there been a basement, Kim would not have burned her hand on an exposed pipe laid in the middle of the household's daily-used space—the hot-water heater and furnace would have been where such things belong—out of sight, out of the way.

Had there been adequate storage space, Mary would not have barked her shin on Chip's tricycle. Had there been

"Hi! What's for chow?"

ample play space in the bedrooms, or anywhere else indoors, Mary and Gladys might have been able to conduct
a rational conversation in some form other than frenetic
shouts over the children's noise. Or, the ladies might have
surrendered the living room to the children and retreated
either to the kitchen or dining room—had there been space
enough in the kitchen; had there been a dining room apart
from the living room. It is not fantastic to suggest that
Gladys' and Mary's conversation would have been considerably shorter if it had been possible to conduct it in better
circumstances; hence, Mary's housework might have had a
better chance to get done before John came home.

Mary observed, without consciously acknowledging the
thought, that her living room had all the cozy privacy of
a railroad station waiting room. To go to the trains, to come
from the trains, to go to the public lavatories, to buy a magazine, to get a bite to eat, you have to cross the waiting room.
Likewise, to go anywhere or do anything in the Drones'
house, the living room must be entered, left, or crossed.
Open the front door and you're in the Drones' living room.
To go from kitchen to bedroom you go through the living
room. Once a file of children came in the Drones' back
kitchen door, unbidden.

"We have to go to the bathroom," their leader told Mary.
"Don't worry. We know where it is. It's the same place as
ours."

And off they went, around the L, through the living room
to the bath.

When the Drones entertained, they entertained in the
living room. The dining alcove was simply too small to seat
six adults. Thus, Mary Drone's infrequent supper parties—
just like every other development wife's supper parties—

were necessarily buffets, featuring casseroles placed on the dining alcove table. Guests helped themselves, then retired to the living room to balance plates on their knees as they perched on the peculiar furniture that seems to come sooner or later to every development house.

John and Mary had an argument about that furniture. John lost. They sold the big, comfortable things—hand-me-downs, slightly gone to seed—that had filled their Jubal Early apartment. Another generation's chattels didn't seem to look right in the new house—they made it seem even smaller than it was. So Mary opened her first charge account and filled her home with the popular new furniture—chairs that looked as though someone had stretched canvas across the threshing legs of an upside-down iron spider; sacroiliac-twisting coffee tables that seemed an inch off the deck; a square box of an easy chair that ended below the small of anyone's back; vague, light chairs made of that vague, blond wood. Somehow, this seemed just right for Mary's new home, and who is to say it was not? *De gustibus non est disputandum,* and besides, everyone else had it. The total effect, however, was to make dining in a Rolling Knolls living room a contortionist's nightmare.

And then, of course, dear little Chip and Kim would come into the living room in their cute pajamas and all the guests would clutch their plates in both hands and smile vacantly and admire the children, and Mary would grin her tight little grin used for such occasions and shoo the children back to bed with advice to forget the noise and just try to go to sleep.

In short, the inadequacy of Mary Drone's house irritated her and bored her and stifled her and led her to occasional shrieks at John, who had no idea the house was turning his wife into a nag. How could he? Mary never told him, because she had never figured it out for herself—not consciously. And John couldn't see the reasons because, for one thing, he didn't live in the house. He left in the morning, came home at night for supper and bed, lounged around over the weekends, and remained completely oblivious of the nature of Mary's days. But other men were not so blind. In fact, serious men were aware of the built-in dangers of the postwar development house as soon as the first one came poking up out of the bulldozed slime.

Back in 1948, Dr. Charles Winslow, widely-known public health authority and professor-emeritus of Yale University's public health school, denounced the "inferior type of small house being provided by speculative builders to meet the veteran demand," and correctly predicted "families living in these houses might suffer serious mental and physical ills."

Dr. Winslow went on to tell the American Institute of Architects, meeting in Salt Lake City that June, that the $10,000–$15,000 houses were "doll houses which out-slum the slummiest of our prewar slums," and said their interior space was "far short of any reasonable minimum" and failed to offer a satisfactory environment for the family. The postwar house, he said, was too small to entertain guests, it lacked sufficient storage space, had poorly-lighted dining alcoves placed in the path of major circulation, lacked space anywhere for children's playcorners, and its bedrooms lacked privacy.

Such houses, he said, were examples of poor design, and he suggested that government subsidization of low-rent housing was the only sane solution to the immediate postwar housing need.

The government, however, wasn't listening to advice of

public health experts or to architects. The government view was "to adopt the view of the builders and ignore the views of the architects," as Howard Moise of Berkeley, California, told the meeting Dr. Winslow addressed.

The government still wasn't listening in March 1950, when T. H. Robsjohn-Gibbings, designer and author, concluded it was "high time" modern houses got back to the business of housing human beings, and charged the nation's architects had been victims of a strict building pattern that reduced their individuality to zero.

In 1951, a year before the veterans housing scandals culminated in the Teague committee report, the *New York Times* was taking a long, hard look at the national housing picture.

"The bald fact is," the *Times* snapped, "that there are too many inadequate houses going up in the suburbs of New York and almost every other city." The paper argued that despite the come-on gimmicks and gadgets, such as the Formica-topped sink and the big BIG *BIG* picture window, "in size, stereotyped design, repetitive floor layouts, the average house leaves much to be desired." The *Times* complained that builders, with just a little "thought and ingenuity," could, at no expense to themselves, offer so much more to the buyer. Of course, the only trouble here was that the builders had used up all their ingenuity when they figured out the wording of the sales contracts.

The extent of the Federal Government's concern with these matters seemed to take the form of the speech Mr. Raymond Foley, then head of the Housing and Home Finance Agency, made to a convention of the National Association of Home Builders. He said "we have overemphasized the two-bedroom house." He suggested the builders might consider reducing their prices by taking smaller profits. For some reason, Mr. Foley's suggestion was not immediately and enthusiastically accepted. He was not borne out of the hall on the shoulders of a delirious throng.

Instead, the nation's building pattern simply drifted from worse to worse, and in 1953 Robert Woods Kennedy, distinguished architect and writer, noted that government housing "by means of a universally-agreed-upon euphemism, is known as 'private.' The private speculator expects and is expected to bleed housing for all it is worth. As in the early days of railroading, factory management, food, advertising, lumbering and farming, so in homes; long-term values are not considered worth worrying about. The worst speculators do not even build a sound house. They have not yet developed a sense of social responsibility. Sooner or later, as has happened in so many other fields, home builders may have their own kind of Pure Food and Drug Act rammed down their throats—but not until the situation has been seen in its true light, as a waste of natural resources and as a menace to the public's emotional health."[1]

Among the factors affecting Mary's emotional health were her memories of other living conditions. Like John Drone, she had spent part of her youth in one of the big, three-story family houses on Elm Street. It might have been difficult to heat and hard to clean, but it did have space. It sheltered three generations of a family; granted privacy to age, play space to youth, offered hospitality to guests and—in sum—satisfied the needs of every person dwelling therein. If the Elm Street house seemed a somewhat inefficient machine for living, nevertheless *living* is what hap-

[1] Robert Woods Kennedy, *The House* (Reinhold, N. Y., 1953).

pened within its comfortable walls. Compared to the big houses on Elm Street, the California Cape Cod Ramblers of Rolling Knolls were so many ill-made, inefficient machines for insufficient existence.

Of course, when John and Mary needed living space at war's end, they were in no position to pick and choose. They had to take what was offered within their means, and, as we've seen, a combination of ruthless circumstances had thrust them into Rolling Knolls. On the day Mary inspected the sample house, her first thoughts were that the one-floor plan and general compactness would make housework quick and simple. With the drudgery done, the rest of her day could be a lilting song.

"It only takes two hours to clean," the salesman had said.

Well, it might have, at that. Despite the foul design of the rambler that didn't ramble, Mary's day might have been considerably more bearable than it was—but only if her house had not been built in Rolling Knolls. In development life, other forces than the shape of the specific dwelling help to shape the dweller. To see these forces at work, let's visit Mary again, on a clear day. Let's visit her on a sunny Tuesday:

The dishes are dry, the beds are made, the children fresh and scrubbed, and woman's work is done until lunch and nap time. It is one minute before 11 A.M. What lilting air will Mary sing? Specifically, what is there to do with her free time in Rolling Knolls?

She can take her children out to play. Only this, and nothing more.

And where will she take them?

Why—to the front lawn, of course. There is no other place. There is no park in Rolling Knolls or near it. There

is no school- or churchyard, no community center. Mary has
no car. The shopping center is two miles away; the bus
stop, one mile away. Mary will therefore take her children
out to play on the tiny lawn just like everyone else.

And so—she did.

At precisely the same moment Mary stepped out of her
door on our sample Tuesday, Gladys Fecund, Henrietta
Spleen, Maryann Faint, Jane Amiable and Eve Wild emerged
from their houses with their children. Mrs. H. Ardis Voter,
who had no child, waited until 11:03 to see whose lawn it
was that day—it troubled her that she'd forgotten. It was
Eve's day, a matter which may require brief explanation.

In the earliest days of Rolling Knolls, there had been no
pattern to what was to become the Every Morning Baby-
sitting Lawn Date. Women simply emerged with their children and nodded to one another, but after a fortnight, clots
of women began to form on lawns. They'd stand and talk
while gusts of children eddied around them.

The first step toward regular lawn-dating began when
Eve Wild, a rather intense young thing, thought of bringing
a folding canvas chair. From that point, the rest is history.
Everyone brought out canvas chairs, and, inevitably, refresh-
ments were offered.

It was Jane Amiable who one morning said, "Oh, let's
all have a bite to eat!" She scampered inside, reappearing
instants later with a tray that must have taken her an hour
to prepare. Naturally, Gladys had said as the company
parted, "You'll all have to come to my lawn tomorrow."

And so it began. It spread like any other contagion. By
tacit consent, Jane had Wednesdays, Gladys staked out a
claim on Thursdays, and other weekdays fell to the lot of
other ladies. Only Mrs. Voter escaped, for she had no child.

"I put Jackson on the pot as soon as I saw him start to fidget," Gladys was telling Jane when Mary Drone arrived at Eve's on our sample Tuesday. "I kept him there a good ten minutes. Finally I decided he wasn't going to go, so I lifted him off and he went all over me and the bathroom."

"I know just how it is," Jane said. "I don't know what I'm going to do with Belinda. We were over at Mother's the other day and Belinda went right on the couch. It came out around the edges of her diaper—all sticky. It was simply awful. Mother asked me—in the nicest way, really, that's what made it so awful—when I thought I'd start Belinda's toilet training."

"I put Abel on the pot every morning as soon as he wakes up," Eve said. "Sometimes he goes and sometimes he doesn't. Sometimes it's too late. But I think he's getting the idea."

"My Gus was all trained at eighteen months," Henrietta Spleen said, and a general silence ensued.

It was Mrs. Voter who, as a neutral, was able to shift the conversation to a slightly less scatological subject—the gross inadequacy of the human male.

"That plaster has been cracked since we moved in do you think Myhusband would fix it?" she rattled. "He did not he got up on a chair two weeks ago and looked at it that's all that happened I finally got on the telephone and the plasterers will be here tomorrow."

"I wanted Buster to put up a towel rack for the children," Gladys testified. "I went out and bought it for him, screws and all, and gave it to him and told him where I wanted it. Days went by. Every night it was either 'I'll do it later, I want to read the paper now,' or it was 'first thing Saturday morning,' and when Saturday came, he'd say, 'A man needs a rest *sometime*.' I guess I'll have to put the rack up myself."

"Men," Henrietta said, "have no idea what we go through."

. . . a slightly less scatological subject . . .

From bitter experience, Mary Drone could predict the future path of the morning's conversation. She hadn't joined in the toilet-training perorations for two reasons: she was dead tired of the subject and (perhaps because she still had a subconscious foot in Elm Street) it seemed somehow indelicate. But even less did she relish the prospect of another Judgment On Husbands. There seemed to her no more viciously divisive influence on suburban marriages than the regular morning polemic. Mankind, it appeared, was divided into two parts. First, there was My Jerk Of A Husband, and second, The Boy I Almost Married. Naturally, the first was mentioned in the tone of a curse; the second, with a sigh.

On this particular Tuesday, Mary's predictions ran true to

form. Mrs. Voter proclaimed woman educated, emancipated, and undeserving of the status of nursemaid and household drudge. Such a status might have been all very well for everyone's grandmother, but it was certainly not the niche for which modern woman was trained. Husbands must be made to realize this and do their share of the work, she said. Not just repair work, but help with the children, dishes, floors and beds. Her Phi Beta Kappa key, Mrs. Voter said resentfully, was hung over the sink.

It was the general testimony that husbands did nothing to ease womankind's intolerable burden of chores, and when Eve untactfully suggested her Adam was simply wonderful about fixing things around the house, there was another of those impolite silences.

But it didn't last long.

"The doctor says it's all Myhusband's fault we can't have a baby the doctor told us what to do and Myhusband tries," Mrs. Voter said contemptuously. "We try once every month Myhusband says he just can't get interested if he knows he *has* to and so it never goes right."

Mrs. Voter paused for breath, a tactical mistake, for Gladys stepped quickly to the rostrum.

"I wish sometimes Buster wouldn't try so much," she said. "We're always succeeding and this month I missed my time again. I've had twins in my family and the doctor says we've a good chance for twins ourselves, and honestly, where do you think we'd put them?"

Eve was silent. But she eyed Mrs. Voter curiously, with something of a speculative gleam in her green eyes.

Henrietta Spleen frankly said she wished she could trade husbands wih Mrs. Voter—a remark which, for once, everyone heard. Heretofore, it seemed to Mary the silent members had been not an audience, but members of a debating society, each thinking of what she would say when her chance came.

"Just for a month," Henrietta said primly. "The doctor says I need a rest."

This opened the floor to a rousing discussion of the unthinking sexual callousness of the husband, called for vivid personal testimony in detail, and Mary felt a regular morning sickness rising in her—a morning sickness that had nothing to do with pregnancy. It was a sickness she'd been feeling every sunny day for the last several weeks. Its medical name is ennui. She gathered Chip and Kim and made her unheard adieux.

Meanwhile, the sacrifice of the husband raged on, unabated. The good ladies of Rolling Knolls hotted the fire higher and higher, lashed themselves into a perfect frenzy against the men who'd betrayed them into matrimony. By the time they went their several ways to put their get to bed, the ladies' eyes were snapping, their pulses racing; their lips were icy slits. If any fool of a husband had showed himself in that neighborhood at that time, his life wouldn't have been worth a Roosevelt dollar.

On her way home from Eve's lawn, Mary wondered how they did it. It always amazed her. Mrs. Spleen wasn't speaking to Mrs. Wild, of course. The Spleens were suing the Wilds for playing their radio too loud at night and cutting the lawn on Sunday mornings, and Mr. Voter was reported to have said, as a lawyer, that the Spleens could win.

For that matter, Henrietta wasn't speaking to Mary, either, because Mary had sent five-year-old Gus home for digging in the Drones' yard last Saturday.

Of course, everyone hated the Spleens—Henrietta for her

imaginary sicknesses, George for his frozen-faced manners. Everyone knew the Spleens shouted at each other and beat their child, just as everyone thought Buster and Gladys Fecund were probably a trifle common because they had all those children and you know how young Gladys must have been when she was married. . .

And everyone was disgusted with the Wilds. Adam didn't water his lawn when everyone else did, and he didn't keep it well cut, but that didn't matter half as much as that back yard of his. Adam parked his truck right in front of the house, too. Most people thought he should leave his truck somewhere else—it smelled so. Adam ran the County Squire Tidy Service, and collected everyone's trash and garbage for miles around. His back yard was a fright, because he used it to store salvaged toilet seats, broken radiators and other odds and ends of contractors' debris waiting ultimate haulage to city junk dealers. But Adam's really unforgivable sin, in the eyes of every woman in the block, was getting that automatic dryer for Eve.

Mary knew Jane Amiable and Gladys Fecund hadn't been speaking. Mary knew how exasperated Jane had been when Gladys had asked her to mind the children while Gladys went shopping. Maryann Faint wasn't speaking to Mrs. Voter because Lawrence Faint had voluntarily withdrawn from Mr. Voter's car pool and nobody knew yet what that was all about.

The wonder of it all was, Mary thought, that women who weren't speaking to one another nevertheless gathered each morning for the regular lawn date, victims of relentless habit and the fact that there was nothing else to do. But Mary should not have worried her once pretty head about who was speaking to whom. The ladies *weren't* speaking to each other—they were speaking to themselves. Another woman's lawn was something like the neutral corner of a prize ring, and the ladies used it as a kind of combination psychiatric couch, confessional, Oxford Movement, and Alcoholics Anonymous. Unlike these estimable institutions, however, the neutral lawn failed to give relief, for like everything else about Rolling Knolls, it was steeped in stifling monotony.

And, there was no escape.

On decent days, children had to be taken out for play and an airing. Since everyone had children, everyone went outside, for no child in Rolling Knolls was old enough to play unwatched. Since the lawns were tiny, and the houses built cheek-by-jowl, everyone met outside. Someone said children make the best neighbors, but surely this means only that children in closely-built communities involve their mothers with one another. Unless Mary Drone locked herself and her children in her inadequate house she lived, perforce, in a world of women and children.

Moreover, she lived only too close to her neighbors. She was discovering something our elder British cousins have remarked at length—that proximity breeds more ills than such simple plagues as typhus and cholera. Proximity also breeds familiarity, and familiarity breeds contempt. In 1953, a group of English sociologists led by Leo Kuper published *Living in Towns,* a study of postwar housing development in bombed-out Coventry. Dr. Kuper's interviewers concluded that the best neighbor is a distant one, as may be judged from these sample statements from British housewives:

"You don't want them [neighbors] always on your hearthstone"; "We could have been good friends if we'd been a bit farther apart"; "We began to feel on top of one another and we quarreled, and that makes things difficult when you're living near together."

Dr. Kuper and his associates formed a rule: that extreme proximity forces neighbors to adjust to one another, willy-nilly, and if adjustment is impossible, one of the neighbors will move. In one case, a family unable to stick their Coventry neighbors any longer moved to another neighborhood even though they had to pay fifty per cent more rent, and even though their move meant the husband had to work Saturdays, Sundays, holidays and overtime every night.

American sociologists, too, have begun to make notes on development life.

"In these communities," said Harold Mendelsohn of American University's Bureau of Social Research, "there is no real privacy. The women become involved in one another's emotional problems. And, unless they take part in community activities, they are apt to be shunned and lead incredibly lonely lives, surrounded by the endless monotony of the development itself and trying to cope with the monotony of their children and housework. Their husbands may drive off to the city each day, but for the women, there is no escape. It's often a tough life for them. . ."

On our clear, sunny, sample Tuesday, Mary Drone, desperately bored by toilet-training, deeply discouraged by the daily attack on the inadequacy of husbands (a matter she knew only too well), retreated into her tiny house and forced the warped door shut. Mechanically, she prepared lunch and put the children down for their naps. Moved by subconscious need, she lowered the venetian blinds across her picture window to shut out the ghastly view of the mirror of her empty life staring at her across the treeless, unpaved street. Listlessly, she picked up a woman's magazine and began to read. The story concerned a gay, bubbling young creature who, whilst engaged in her secretarial duties, fell in love with the darkly handsome stockroom clerk, not knowing he was really a director of the firm working in disguise.

Later that afternoon—after romance had culminated in marriage, a stately Long Island home and, therefore, happiness—Mary's children woke from their naps and Mary began to think of supper, John's return, and her evening. Supper would have to be something simple; she'd make it out of cans.

Mary took down a prepared spaghetti dinner from her shelves, a can of peas, and, casting around for dessert, decided on mixed fruit. She emptied the spaghetti and the peas into saucepans, put the saucepans on the stove; emptied the canned fruit into a bowl and put the bowl in the refrigerator. Then she ran a tub of water and, leaving the door ajar so that she could keep an ear out for her children, shed her shirt and bluejeans and bathed.

Then she dressed in perfume, blouse, silk stockings, tweed skirt, dark shoes and bracelets. In three other Rolling Knolls estates, three other chatelaines underwent similar ablutions. Gladys, Maryann, Jane and Mary were making themselves fresh and lovely, not for their husbands, but for each other, for Tuesday evenings meant bridge at Maryann's. Indeed, when Buster, Lawrence, Henry and John returned to their manors, their ladies denied them the perfunctory, sterile, connubial kiss—"You'll smear my lipstick," each lady said.

Four husbands did the dishes and put the children to bed, while four wives that evening confused Goren with Blackwood and discussed babies and the characters of absent neighbors. And once again, Mary felt caught in a deadly trap.

The real nature of the trap was this: Mary had fallen into a world of women without men. She had moved into a house that could never be a home. She had moved into a neighborhood that could never be a community. She had moved into a strange, new way of life—a kind of life America had never seen before.

In the old Elm Street neighborhoods of this nation, both in small towns and large, the houses are each different from the other, inhabited by people of differing ages, occupations, dress, manners and beliefs. The houses, sufficient to meet the needs of each of their inhabitants, are centers of family life. In Elm Street, one housewife did not necessarily meet—or even necessarily know—all other housewives on the block. For one thing, the housewives of Elm Street might well have little in common.

In Elm Street the husband still plays more or less his traditional role in the family. Thus, an Elm Street wife's social acquaintances were often those introduced by her husband. Going out of an evening most usually meant going to the home of a husband's friend. And, while the husband's friends might share a common business neighborhood, they most certainly did not share a common residential neighborhood, much less the same residential block. Therefore, an Elm Street woman's social life was apt to carry her to different parts of town, to homes different in detail from her own. Such variety lent richness and perspective to her own life.

In Rolling Knolls, however, there were no husbands. Men were overnight lodgers or casual weekend guests. They left each morning for the city, which satisfied their need for change and the society of others. When they came home at night, they were apt to want to stay there. They seldom visited their business acquaintances socially, for such acquaintances might well live miles away in some other development at the far end of the metropolitan sprawl. Husbands came to Rolling Knolls as they came to the Jubal Early Homes, to eat and sleep, and when they left in the morning, ownership of Rolling Knolls passed by default to a matriarchy.

Thus the women assumed the lead in development social life. They introduced their friends to their husbands. And, because they were all anchored close to their inadequate houses by the needs of their young children, their friends were necessarily one another. Their friendships were recruited entirely within their neighborhood block. Thus, the lawn date in the morning. Thus, the bridge date in the evening. And always with the same people—people horribly like themselves.

It is a hideous travesty to suggest the housewives of Rolling Knolls had "something in common" when the bitter truth is they had only too much in common. It is true that the dwelling shapes the dweller. When all dwellings are the same shape, all dwellers are squeezed into the same shape. Thus, Mary Drone in Rolling Knolls was living much closer in every way to 1984 than to 1934, for she dwelt in a vast, communistic, female barracks. This communism, like any other, was made possible by destruction of the individual. In this case, destruction began with obliteration of the individualistic house and self-sufficient neighborhood, and from there on, the creation of mass-produced human beings followed as the night the day. The job was done quickly enough, for Rolling Knolls dwellers mostly came that way.

George Spleen at thirty-two was the oldest man in the neighborhood; John Drone, at twenty-four, the youngest. Mrs. Voter, thirty-three, was the matriarch, and Gladys

Fecund's twenty years fitted her for the role of neighborhood ingénue. Likewise, the income range of Rolling Knolls families fluctuated within one thousand dollars; all but Adam Wild were salaried office workers. Since everyone patronized the one closest shopping center, Rolling Knolls houses were furnished alike, their shelves were stocked with the same supermarket's drab fare, every woman used *The Joy of Cooking*, and everyone bought the same plastic reproduction of an African carving for the identical living-room casual table. A visiting anthropologist would have remarked on the uniformity of the male office costume, on the popularity of red denim slacks among the ladies. On summer days, Rolling Knolls was a waterless Riviera of T shirts and khaki slacks, of halters, shorts and sandals. If there was a community problem—such as the lack of paved streets—everyone shared it, in anger. And if there was any trifle of community gossip, everyone shared that, too. Considering the circumstances, it was only logical that gossip concerned variations from the norm, such as the Wilds' habit of kissing in public. When Adam return from his labors, Eve rushed from the house to meet him, and he'd lift her to him, and she kissed him with lips and tongue and all of her. Eve didn't play bridge.

Mark Twain had something to say on this dreary subject of homogenous communities. He sent an old sea captain, Captain Stormfield, off to Heaven at the end of his days. Captain Stormfield checked in and drew his wings, halo and harp from commissary and set out for the nearest cloud bank. He had a little difficulty with take-offs and landings, couldn't sing, and didn't know beans about a harp, and the more he considered the proposition, the less he liked it. Further, he'd assumed everyone in Heaven had perpetual youth, but frankly, he died old, and the half-baked chitchat of twenty-one-year-olds bored him. Then, when things were looking blackest, Captain Stormfield had a happy surprise. Through a friend, he discovered Heaven wasn't necessarily an homogenous, youthful, celestial choir. A man could be what he wished in Heaven—based of course on the stuff inside him —and Captain Stormfield went very earnestly back to the business of being himself—an individual. He found this to be a general rule; that Heaven was various and many-colored after all. He therefore turned in his wings, halo and harp and settled down to the blissful prospect of never-ending variety. Hell, he decided, was homogenous.

Mary Drone, however, was in a completely different position. She'd left Elm Street's prewar Heaven to fall smack into Samuel O. Burmal's jerry-built, homogenous, postwar Hell. It was an even coarser jest of Fate that Mary was plunged into this ridiculous environment precisely at the worst of all possible times of her life.

As all women have long known, and as many men are coming to suspect, a young wife saddled with sole responsibility for house and preschool children is a slave in a twenty-four-hour-shift salt mine. More than anything else in this bountiful world, she needs loving consideration, recreation, rest and healthful change. In Mary Drone's case, her young husband—like other development husbands— hadn't the vaguest clue that everyday monotony was crushing Mary's spirit into the shape of a dessicated persimmon. In fact, the women didn't know it themselves. Romances in the ladies' magazines, in movies, advertisements and novels all had conditioned the ladies to think marriage meant children, homes of their own, and happiness. Now, if life seemed a little sour, surely it was not the fault of house or children. Therefore, they inveighed against their absent husbands by day and were indifferent to them at night, and thus they sealed off one avenue that might have led to the loving consideration they so badly needed.

Furthermore, the ladies of Rolling Knolls could not turn to relatives in their hours of need. The houses were not large enough for two generations, let alone three, and anyway, everyone's parents lived hundreds of miles away in the various Elm Streets of the land. Few indeed were the Rolling Knolls housewives whose parents or aunts lived near-by and could baby-sit to permit the housewife the welcome hour of rest or change that a day in the city could afford. But worst of all the factors that seared the female soul was the terrifying monotony of Rolling Knolls itself.

If Mary did not take part in the morning lawn date, but chose to take a morning stroll with her children instead, where would she go, and what would she see?

She would leave her house, turn the corner of Kasserine Pass, move in a trance up Kasserine to Midway, down Midway to Salerno, down Salerno to Iwo Jima, and so find her way back to Bataan. And not once would the view change. Not once, in any slightest way.

Each identical house, with its identical picture window, with its identical dwarf cedars, the identical gullies in the eroding lawns, always the same, the same, the same, row on row, would not inspire Mary's personal skylark to pour forth its full heart in profuse strains of unpremeditated art.

And there was no way out.

Rolling Knolls was neither city nor country, but a combination of the disadvantages of both. There was no focus of community interest; hence Rolling Knolls was not a community in the sociological sense. There was, as noted, no church, no school, no park, no corner store. There was not

the slightest recreational facility of any kind for either
mother or child. There were only a lot of houses. To walk
down Elm Street was an experience, but to walk through
Rolling Knolls was to move somnambulistically through
Limbo, until finally, there came a house like all the other
houses, but which Mary could realize was home by the black
13 on the warped white doorframe.

By this time, it should not astonish the fascinated reader
to discover that Mary's Tuesday evening bridge game followed the pattern of all other Tuesday evening bridge games
at Maryann's. Bridge, naturally, was not the overwhelming
interest of the evening. The cards were mere vehicles for
familiar conversations. Every woman, feeling the pressure of
social forces quite beyond her ken, imagined the way to
personal salvation was paved with gold.

Specifically, each said she thought life would be ever so
much better if only John, or Henry, or Lawrence, or Buster
earned a little more money.

"I could certainly use a dryer like Eve Wild's," Mary said.
"Yesterday it rained and I had to hang the wash inside again.
It was the third Monday in a row that it's rained. I could
certainly use a dryer, but honestly, I don't know where the
money will come from."

"I want Buster to get me a car as soon as this awful shortage lets up," Gladys said. "Adam Wild has a car. He drives
that smelly truck all day, and leaves the car home for Eve
to drive. But you know, she almost never uses it."

"Eve likes it here," Maryann said with faint disbelief
"You'd think she'd offer to take somebody out for a drive,
wouldn't you?"

"What I want someday," Jane said, "is all my furniture
re-covered."

It seemed they all had wants. They wanted new drapes, rugs, lamps, and gadgets, gadgets, gadgets—led, of course, by that be-all, end-all gadget of our time, the automobile.

The ladies could speak freely, for there was no man to hear. After meeting his wife's guests, Lawrence Faint had obediently retired to the bedroom, to read in bed.

The ladies chattered on about their needs, confusing things for experiences. What would an automatic dryer do for Mary? To what extent would new drapes enlighten Jane's days? It would have been far more sensible for the ladies to have considered hiring women once a week to mind the children while they went window-shopping in the city. For the price of a dryer, Mary could have purchased a year's worth of once-a-week vacations, and there's no doubt she would have been a happier woman for it.

But Mary was young and inexperienced, and so were her neighbors, and there were no elders in Rolling Knolls to teach life's lessons through advice or example. The Tuesday night bridge game broke up, like others before it and others to come, on a note of mutual discontent.

"Have a nice time?" John Drone asked sleepily as his Mary came to bed.

"Why don't we get a car?" Mary demanded.

"Hmm?"

"I said, why don't you get me an automatic dryer and get us a car?"

"With what?" John asked, coming fully awake.

"Oh, nothing. Go back to sleep," Mary said.

"Aw, honey, we just can't do it," John said. "The streets will be paved next week, and we'll have that street assessment coming up; it's all we can do to swing this house, as it is."

Mary said nothing.

"We won't always be making fifty dollars a week," John said in exactly the same tone he'd always said this. "I'm trying. You know I am. I'm going to take the Civil Service exam for junior executive next week. If I pass it . . . if I pass it, I'll put our name down for a used car."

Mary, who could have said something, remained silent. She turned her back to John in utter finality. John put a tentative hand on her shoulder.

"Not tonight," Mary decided for him. "I'm tired, and so are you."

Then, another day ended, she pressed her head against the pillow and wet the pillow with silent tears. How many days like this would there be in her life? The mortgage had nineteen and a half years to run. She drifted off to exhausted sleep.

John, wakened now, lay on his back with his side lightly touching his wife's turned back, and considered his future. If he passed the test, the job he had in mind might well be his for the asking. His veteran's preference gave him a good chance. More than anything else, John Drone, Census Bureau file clerk, coveted the post of assistant division chief in charge of pencil procurement for the Bureau's Division of Miscellaneous Statistics.

If he passed the test, he might put his name down on a waiting list for a car, at that. All in all, he felt pretty good. He was young, had a chance to rise, had a good wife and two fine kids, and a new house of his own. . .

4. Onward and Downward

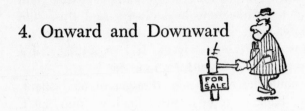

"These neighborhoods accentuate the problems."
—Miss Elizabeth O'Malley, Director, Montgomery
County, Maryland, Social Service League

ON A DAY all soft and bright as only spring days can be, a day full of early warmth and the good smell of earthy promise, Lawrence Faint staggered out of his house bent beneath the unwieldy weight of a clothes tree. It was his intention to plant it in the red clay of his freehold at Rolling Knolls. He wrestled it to the ground, and then straightened, perspiring slightly. Now he needed a shovel. It was a Saturday. John Drone would be home, and John might just have a shovel. If not Drone, then Amiable, or—certainly—Wild. But John's was the closest house.

"Shovel?" John repeated. "Oh, sure. I think we have one. Come in, Larry, while I ask Mary."

"It's with the rake, under Chip's bed, next to the wall, behind the suitcases," Mary called from the bathroom.

"I'll give you a hand," John told Faint, and ten minutes later excavation was under way. Engrossed in their work, they did not notice Mrs. Voter's approach behind them.

"Does that shovel have tape on the handle?" she demanded. "Myhusband loaned his shovel to someone and can't remember who we've never gotten it back but we had tape on the handle so we'd know it's ours."

"Hello," John said. "Good morning. No, I think this one is mine—see, there's no tape on the handle. It's an old shovel; I think I got it at the surplus store in town."

"Well, I don't know what happened to ours," she said. And then, dismissing the mystery of the missing tool, she turned to Lawrence Faint.

"What are you doing you're not going to put that clothes tree there are you? My kitchen window looks down through all these back yards and I certainly don't think it's a bit nice to have to look out of the house into a yard full of wash hanging out to dry if we're going to make these yards a big, landscaped play area for everyone we can't put up things like that why don't you put it around on the side of your house where it will be out of the way?"

"Gosh, there's no sun on the side," Faint said.

"Well, why don't you put it around front?"

"I guess we cou . . . well, gee, it wouldn't look good around there, either," Faint said awkwardly. "Anyway, we'll take it right down when the clothes are dry, and they'll dry fast it's such a nice day.

"See?" he went on. "We're going to put this metal socket in the ground, and the clothes tree slips into the socket, so you can take it up when you're not using it."

Mrs. Voter was one of the few women in this world who could successfully sniff. She sniffed. Then she rounded on Drone, spearing him with her bright, beady eyes.

"When are you going to plant rosebushes?" she wanted to know.

"Oh, sometime, I guess," said Drone, who never in his

life had contemplated planting a rosebush. He guessed it was something Mary had discussed with Mrs. Voter.

"I'd like to know what happened to our shovel," Mrs. Voter said, sniffed, and marched away.

"What was that all about?" Faint asked, staring at Mrs. Voter's tweedy back.

"I think," John said, "she's been talking to the women about getting everybody to agree not to put up fences, and to make all the yards enclosed by Iwo Jima, Bataan, Kasserine and Midway into a big play area. She asked Mary if we'd put up the swings, in our yard."

"You mean swings for *all* the kids in *your* yard?"

"Yeah. Mrs. Voter said we could have the swings, and somebody else could have the jungle gym and another person the sandbox area, and so on."

"And what was she going to have in her yard?"

"A garden, she said. She said she doesn't have any kids, you know."

"Is she crazy?" Faint asked seriously.

"I think she just means well," John said.

And they planted the clothes tree in silence.

Mrs. Voter was on absolutely unassailable ground in her suggestion that Rolling Knolls, lacking any recreational facility or any park, must do what it could with its back yards. But she carried to a point of genius the ability to present her arguments in the worst possible manner, and to irritate those whose help she needed. Furthermore, she completely misunderstood the pattern of social relationships within a housing development. She can be excused this latter fault, however, for housing developments are a new world, one in which sociologists are just becoming profoundly interested. There is little literature on the subject and Mrs. Voter, after all, had no more experience than anyone else with the odd new way of life that is busily growing up around our cities, all across the nation.

The first and most important fact to realize about housing development neighbors is that they are not really friends. They can never be friends; the best relationship they can achieve with one another is a superficial acquaintance based on service needs. Harold Mendelsohn, American University sociologist, put it thus:

"In housing developments patterns emerge which make for superficial cohesiveness. It is entirely artificial, based on providing mutual conveniences, rather than on a basis of friendship, or on a basis of fundamental needs. A wants a hammer. He borrows one from B. If he is feuding with B, it makes no difference, he'll borrow one from C. D and E get into a mutual baby-sitting agreement. There is a car pool. All these are conveniences, just service needs. A man in a development has no need to socialize with the other men; his socializing takes place in the city where he works. Therefore, development men are apt to nod to one another, or borrow things from one another, and their relationships in borrowing hammers, say, are no deeper than the relationships you have with the man who comes to fix the plumbing in a city apartment. The development women socialize because they can't escape one another—they're always out on the lawns with their children and the children play together and therefore the mothers meet. But most of *their* acquaintance is based on service needs—the borrowed cup of sugar; the spoonful of cornstarch for baby's sore bottom. They merely supply services to one another—the same services a city would normally supply through its stores and delivery services.

"Moreover," Mr. Mendelsohn said, "these people lack a

basis of deep friendships with one another. They are too much alike in age, jobs, number of children, and so on. Normally, you make friends where you live, or where you work. If you live in a community of people very much like yourselves, the pressure for making friends is great. But in an homogenous community, no one has anything to offer anyone else. What ideas are expressed? What values formed? What do you give to your neighbor? What can he give you?

"Development people," Mr. Mendelsohn answered himself, "have nothing to gain from one another. There is a great deal of neighboring among the women, but no real friendships emerge, for too-much-alike people have nothing to communicate to each other; no fundamentally different ideas are exchanged."

Thus, while Mrs. Voter was easily able to marshal the resources of Rolling Knolls in open warfare against a common enemy to obtain paved streets and new schools and more teachers, it was something else again when she tried to get the neighbors together to create a common play center out of their own back yards. The overwhelming fact was, nobody liked his neighbor sufficiently to want to share a patch of sod with him.

Second, and nearly as important, nobody in Rolling Knolls thought of living there forever—except, perhaps, the Wilds, who would have been deeply content by themselves in a tent pitched in the middle of Union Station. But everyone else thought constantly of moving away at some vague, future time. Meanwhile, they regarded the mortgaged property as their own, and consequently considered "improving it" to increase a future market value. Closest to their needs, but furthest from their thoughts, was Mrs. Voter's dream of a communal back yard. Instead, this is what happened to the free, open areas of Rolling Knolls:

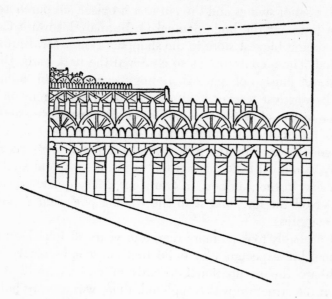

Everybody built fences.

Particularly striking was the arrangement of Iwo Jima Avenue, beginning with the Voters' prim, white, picket fence. Next to it was a heavy fence of criss-crossed, whitewashed planks—a charming arrangement of elongated X's. And then came that fence of whitewashed half-cartwheels, then an iron-wire fence warranted against cyclones, and last, again in white, one that was more a palisade than a row of pickets.

Had it been possible to drive rapidly along the chuckholes of Iwo Jima's newly-poured blacktop, one's eyes would vibrate first up and down, then zigzag, then roll, then blur, and then bounce up and down again as one observed the fences. Only the Wilds lacked a fence.

Meanwhile the back yards were put to use. Into each tiny yard came, in due course, a jungle gym, a sandbox, a wading pool, a set of swings and the outdoor fireplace, all purchased —on time—at the huge Samuel O. Burmal Hardware Co., newest and biggest store in the shopping center Mr. Burmal owned. These contraptions so cluttered the back yards that whatever illusion of space there might have been in Rolling Knolls was lost forever. Only the need for space remained. It is a matter of fact that John Drone, standing up to stretch from the maladroit construction of his outdoor fireplace, crowned himself on the iron bars of the jungle gym, reeled away, stumbled headlong across the swing seat, and landed face first in the sandbox. In two steps, Mary quickly tore a diaper off the line, wet it in the wading pool, and applied the compress.

It probably took no more than four years off John Drone's normal life expectancy to build that outdoor fireplace, but such are the occupational hazards of do-it-yourself. And when the structure was completed, there was a nasty bulge to the back wall and the whole thing had a rakish tilt that gave it considerable local notoriety. Word eventually got back to Drone that George Spleen reportedly said the Drones could make money by selling tickets to see the world's smallest leaning tower. If Spleen really said that, his remark might well have had its origin in the following bit of Rolling Knolls history:

No sooner was the mortar dry than John and Mary Drone invited Jane and Henry Amiable over for a steak scorching.

"We're going to have a real charcoal cook-out in our own fireplace," John said.

"What can we bring?" Jane wanted to know. "Can we bring the salad?"

On that fateful June evening, the Amiables arrived not only with the salad, but with their infants and their large collie, Sandy Mac. They arrived to find John pouring kerosene on charcoal briquettes.

"He's been trying to get a fire going for hours," Mary explained. "Paper wouldn't do at all."

There was a gust of flame and John lurched back.

"There," he said, rubbing his oily hands on his chef's apron. "She'll go now. We'll start cooking as soon as it dies down to embers."

John went indoors, and returned with a huge steak which he showed with considerable pride before he placed it carefully on a stone near his roaring oil blaze.

"I'll get some beer while we're waiting," he said brightly, and skipped inside again.

John had no sooner opened his refrigerator when the sound of canine furor smote his ears. Drone quickly folded a newspaper into a club and raced outside.

For some reason best known to themselves, the Spleens' boxer, Blaze, and the Amiables' Sandy Mac hated one another with livid fury. Blaze had come over the Spleens' fence in a soaring arc of singular beauty, and was now attached by his teeth to Sandy Mac's throat.

Drone waded manfully into the dogfight, clubbed paper raised. And then he paused.

Which dog should he hit?

He couldn't hit the Amiables' dog because the Amiables were his guests. And he couldn't hit Spleen's dog, because Drone had to live next to Spleen for the next twenty years. With the impartial wisdom of Solomon, Drone began to strike first one dog, then the other.

"Why in hell don't you hit that other slob's dog?" Spleen roared, bursting out of his house and vaulting the fence.

"Well . . ." Drone dithered.

"Why don't you keep your damn mutt in your own yard?"
Amiable snapped at Spleen.

Mayhem was prevented only by the presence of the ladies,
and Spleen, dragging Blaze away, left muttering to himself.
When he'd gone, all hands sighed and returned to the interrupted party.

And then they saw it.

Sandy Mac had taken advantage of the diversion to gobble
the steak Drone had laid out near the fire. He was ripping
up the last of it.

Mary recovered first. It was all right, she said, they'd just
have something else instead.

So on that first night of eating out under the kindly shelter
of God's clean June sky, the Drones and the Amiables and
their squirming children swatted bugs and ate salad and
bread and butter, and warmed cans of spaghetti over the
embers, and washed it down with boiled coffee which tasted
faintly of kerosene and charcoal.

The party had far-reaching effects. Next day, not only
were the Spleens not speaking to the Drones or the Amiables,
but it developed the Faints', the Fecunds', and the Voters'
feelings had been hurt because they had not been invited.
The rule is, development dwellers may not form real friendships, but they can, and do, form real enmities on the basis
of imagined snubs. They do it with the speed of light. Thus,
Mary found out at the morning lawn date that if she invited
one Rolling Knolls family to eat with her in public, she would
have to invite the whole block. Everybody understood this
perfectly, and so, out of the chaos of the Drones' first cook-
out, the block party arose—a ghastly phoenix if ever there
was one.

The block party was necessarily a summer thing, for there

was no space in any Rolling Knolls house to entertain more than four people comfortably. Naturally, every Rolling Knolls back yard came to have its outdoor fireplace and, naturally again, it was Mrs. Voter who gave birth to the block party idea.

"We're having a party for the whole neighborhood on Thursday night instead of the Citizens' Association meeting," Mrs. Voter ordained, "so everyone's invited and we'll make a barbecue in our fireplace. Everyone bring something if he wants."

All the rest of that summer, barbecue block party followed barbecue block party, and each party was exactly like all others. The specialty was charred chicken and salad, prepared by some luckless male, and each party fell apart as quickly and completely as an ill-made hollandaise sauce. The women would gather into one tight little clot against one fence, and the men would congeal in another corner, sitting on sandboxes, leaning against jungle gyms. The ladies would resume their toilet-training researches and the men would discuss such safely neutral subjects as automobiles, wartime experiences, and the difference in beers. Everyone left each party wondering why he'd come.

Nothing can endure forever, and it was appropriate that Mrs. Voter should have dealt the block party its death blow. She did it unwittingly, of course. Toward the end of the summer, she gave a barbecue, and midway through the evening someone—it was Spleen, no doubt—began comparing notes all around. It was thereupon discovered the Faints had supplied the chicken, the Amiables the salad, the Drones the sauce, the Spleens the bread and coffee, and the Voters not one blessed thing other than the back yard and the fireplace. The block party was therefore immediately abandoned and did not reappear for years, and then in a wildly different form.

Days dragged into weeks, and weeks into months and just when it seemed nothing could save the Mary Drones of this land from a fate worse than life, television burst upon America. It came to Mary Drone thus:

She was sitting moodily in her kitchen, listening to the racket of her jittering washer, when the phone rang.

"We've got one!" Jane Amiable's excited voice said. "Could you and John come over tonight to watch it with us?"

That evening, after the children were abed, John and Mary knocked at the Amiables' door.

"Shhh!" Jane whispered sharply. "Come in. Find a seat."

In wonder, the Drones entered the Amiables' house as though it were a cathedral. They made their way into the darkened room, bumped into the huddled forms of the Fecunds, and sat gingerly on the rug. At the end of the room, perched on a table, was a tiny box with a picture window. From time to time the picture blurred, or streaked, or skipped merrily up and down, but Henry Amiable squatted constantly below the altar, reaching up to turn the dials, and the show—such as it was—went on.

It reminded John Drone vaguely of something he'd seen once, as a child. He couldn't place it, but the memory he could not name persisted. He was seeing vaudeville once again, this time in microcosm.

During the evening, John and Mary took turns at leaving the room to return to their house to make sure the children were safe and soundly sleeping. And each time they left or entered the Amiables' house, Jane would say "Shhh."

From this point, things moved briskly. Television even

penetrated the fastnesses of Colorado, appeared in the lonely mountain cabins of Tennessee's Cumberland Plateau. But chiefly it swept through the developments, and every house in every Rolling Knolls everywhere acquired a television set, and every television set developed expensive maladies, and a whole new realm of larceny unfolded before the glittering eyes of appliance dealers and repairmen. But that is another story—perhaps another book. We're concerned here with what television did to the lives of development dwellers.

For the first months, a wondrous change was wrought. From seven P.M. on, in those days, there was not a light to be seen in Rolling Knolls. Every house but one was dark, and apparently uninhabited, but within every shuttered living room there gleamed a feeble phosphorescence, a tiny picture flickering in that glow. Over the bewitched community there swelled a common sound. Sometimes it was a fanfare, introducing a commercial. Sometimes it was the thin, jubilant cry of a studio audience in New York wildly cheering a contestant who had just announced he came from Detroit, Michigan. Sometimes it was the dumb-de-dumb-dumb musical signature of a period crime piece. But whatever the sound, it was a common sound, rising above the darkened houses, for everyone watched the same shows.

There is no question that TV, as television became known, at first lifted a great burden from the rounded shoulders of Rolling Knolls housewives. To their infinite joy, they discovered the Twentieth Century's built-in baby-sitter. Or, as Eve Wild (the one woman who refused to have a set in her house) put it in a letter to a friend:

I have just visited a TV house. Now at last I know at first hand why so many people have it. You never know you have any children in the house. They just sit there like a bunch of morons, and I mean morons, with their teeth hanging out, staring. It's just like going on a vacation. You turn all your responsibilities for the children over to somebody else, namely, Walt Disney.

Mary Drone, unwilling and unable to endure the chatter of her neighbors, at first took refuge in her television set. She became aware of Arthur Godfrey. For weeks she watched, fascinated by the rasping chuckles, the strange silences, the peculiar blankness of that pudgy face, the earnest pleadings to buy this and that. She laughed when the studio audience laughed, and at the end of the program she couldn't remember what in the world had seemed so funny. She had the eerie feeling Godfrey was boring, but she watched and listened anyway.

Then came the morning when she gave it up and emerged in defeat to the lawn date.

"I've been watching TV," she apologized to Jane Amiable, completely unaware this was also Jane's first morning out in weeks.

"I kept watching and watching, waiting for something good to come on, and afterwards I wondered why I'd been watching."

"My mother wrote that she'd just got a set," Jane said. "She asked me to tell her what the good programs were, but it turned out we'd been watching the same channels. Do you know what the good programs are? Everybody says there are some good programs on TV."

"I think," Mary said, "they must all come on after we're in bed."

"One thing," Gladys Fecund said, "TV is a godsend for

the children. I turn it on while I'm fixing supper and the kids sit there out of the way and watch."

"No child," Mrs. Voter ruled, "should be allowed to look at the things they have on the children's programs."

This latter point was soon resolved by the children themselves. For months, little glassy eyes stared blank and vacant. Then the kids gave it up as a bad job and went back to play, but not before some special conditioning had set in. It remained for three-year-old Jackson Fecund to sum it up. He was sitting in the living room when the venetian blinds suddenly came rattling down across the picture window.

"Mommy!" he wailed, "Mommy! The picture's lost!"

Television came to be less constantly watched, but in terms of woman-hours on this fair earth, uncounted thousands of lives are still spent in a trance before the tiny screen. Television is the most vivid means of mass communication man has yet devised, and its effect on development life cannot be overemphasized. Again, Mr. Mendelsohn can help us put this thing in proper perspective.

"Lacking stimulation from their neighbors," Mr. Mendelsohn said, "oppressed by ennui, development people turn to the mass-communications media to find new ideas. Then, because everyone sees the same TV shows, reads the same article in the same magazine, they all come up with the same idea at the same time, and the result is more ennui. The communications media, realizing that tremendous numbers of their readers, watchers, and listeners live in developments, have begun to angle their productions for the development public. All this results in less and less variation in taste, and the feeling of ennui is reinforced."

As though determined to prove Mr. Mendelsohn's pudding, Mary Drone watched Folly Gay, America's Lighthearted TV Housekeeper, prepare a Yummy Gummy Surprise from an Empire Mills cake mix. Later that same morning, Mary chatted about Folly's program with Jane, Gladys and Maryann. That evening four ladies prepared themselves for one another, adding white gloves to their costumes, and advised their husbands to baby-sit while they drove to the shopping center. At this bazaar they went their several ways, but at some time in the evening each lady acquired a Yummy Gummy mix, and next day, four families sat down at four separate tables to sample a sticky, sodden goo that Folly Gay had promised "would bring a new, dancing joy to your TV supper—and all you have to do is add water."

Yummy Gummys came in six distinctively similar flavors, of course, and don't think for a moment everyone in Rolling Knolls didn't enjoy each of those six flavors within the week. And so, everyone foundered on Yummy Gummys, and gustatorial boredom set in anew. But by that time, Folly Gay was promising ecstatic new deliriums could be yours, if you simply parlayed twenty-six cents and the white of one egg into an Empire Mills Bubbling Fountain.

But it wasn't just cake mixes. It was gadgets for your outdoor fireplace, it was Hopalong Cassidy preparing the way for Davy Crockett, it was trivets and window drapes and TV hassocks and power mowers and politicians and illustrated lectures on how to do anything from bring up your child to dig your own grave.

Television was the gaudiest of the media, and the most effective, but in all mass-communications media the central idea is to sell things to the mass of listeners, watchers and readers. In developments like Rolling Knolls, a ready-made captive audience awaited the arrival of the two-dimensional snake-oil salesman of our time. As has been suggested, development dwellers are about as unlike one another as the interchangeable parts of a General Motors assembly line, and thus it is not surprising they should watch the same TV programs, read the same books, papers and magazines, and, reacting from the same stimuli, embrace the same suggestions to buy the same things.

This was the great truth upon which merchants of the development shopping centers capitalized. There is a rule which every Harvard Business School student learns at once: "Market is never wrong." Thus, the goods and services available at the shopping center near Rolling Knolls were aimed squarely at the market—at the homogenous market of Rolling Knolls. Hence, it became impossible to buy any but one of three basic designs of trivets at the shopping center's Giftie Shoppe, for the proprietress well knew that to stock a fourth design would burden her inventory with a hopeless item.

Likewise, the supermarket did not (and will not) stock a single item it could not reasonably expect to move from its shelves within a certain time-shelfspace formula; hence all Rolling Knolls meals are identical, for there is no opportunity to experiment in new foods—the supermarket won't stock them. In other words, the only way it becomes possible for the Giftie Shoppe to stop stocking trivets is for New York's advertisers suddenly to plant a new trivet-replacing fad, say colored calabashes, to hang on Rolling Knolls walls. So, the word about calabashes is slipped into magazines and into TV and radio scripts, and trivets join horsecollars on the back shelf, and there's a brisk trade in the same colors of calabashes until the next fad comes around. The process is something like that Indian snake that keeps eating itself tail-first, nourishing and consuming itself at the same time. Mr. Mendelsohn has watched this process with wry, scientific interest.

"In these developments," he said, "the only escape for many people is through the changing fads proclaimed by the mass media. Thirty years ago, the sociology textbooks used to say a fad was a spontaneous expression of popular taste, but today's fads are about as spontaneous as the Great Pyramid. Fads are made up by New York's advertising agencies to sell things. The mass-communications media largely exist on creating synthetic fads to sell more advertising to sell more fads.

"Embracing a fad will provide a momentary gratification," he added, "but it will not provide a solution to the problem of living in a development other than a temporary relief from boredom. Building a fireplace from somebody else's plan, assembling a kit that somebody else has packaged, doing something because you hear over television that somebody else is doing it, does not provide a basic answer to the individual's role in life. And when everybody around you embraces the same fad, the pattern of ennui is reinforced.

"The readiness with which these experiments, these fads, are put into effect reflects the basic boredom of development life.

"You will also find these people turning in on themselves with great care and attention," Mr. Mendelsohn continued. "You not only have Do-It-Yourself, but How To. In How To you go beyond the physical business of how to build your own scaffold and get into this pseudopsychological claptrap —into the spiritual realm. You get books on How To think straight, How To stop worrying, reduce tension, How To be happy, How To keep your daughter from petting, and on and on. How To is just another appendage of Do-It-Yourself, and like Do-It-Yourself, nobody does it himself. Nobody figures out How To. The thinking is all done for you in New York and put into a package and you use it until the next fad comes along, and in the process, individuality, if any, is destroyed.

"These development women," he said, "will get involved in How To bring up their children. Of course, they may well have acute anxiety as to what to do with a kid in a development environment, but their willingness to try out every new fad on their kids is most often just another means of taking up time. Through boredom, they'll experiment in How To with their children."

In short, the good citizens of Rollings Knolls got the full jolt of the mass media's high pressure because it was chiefly designed for them, and there they were, all in one place, set up for the jolt. If they didn't absorb it from TV, they got it from the national magazines, and the whopping result was that the merchants' cash registers began jangling at a furious rate all over America as the first pennies of the down payments came pouring in. And, housing developments being what they are, development dwellers dropped most of the dough into the pockets of those who manufactured gadgets for home improvement or repair.

You might think John Drone's simple lack of money would render him immune from the gadget-buying epidemic that swept through Rolling Knolls. Not a bit of it. John Drone had as much buying power as George Spleen or anyone else, except, possibly, Adam Wild.

"What makes you think we can't afford a TV set?" Mary had demanded after their first television experience at the

Amiables'. "Of course we can. Buy it on time, as the ads say."

"Look," John said, not unreasonably, "it costs more if you buy things that way. You have to pay carrying charges."

"You know perfectly well we will never be able to save enough to afford a TV set," Mary said. "You're buying a house on time, aren't you? I can't see any difference in buying anything else on time."

Unfortunately, John Drone had at last realized his first ambition, which was to become assistant pencil procurement officer for the Census Bureau's Division of Miscellaneous Statistics, so he couldn't plead he was still making fifty dollars a week. He looked at Mary's set face, dithered a bit, and then gave up. The TV set arrived the next day and, as has been suggested, the TV set was merely the hunting license. Next came the secondhand car, the automatic dryer, the dishwasher and dispose-all, the electrical frypans, the new kind of vacuum cleaner.

So the Drones paid more for their gadgets than millionaires would think of paying for the same gadgets, and it would be wonderful to say the gadgets brought tingling gaiety to Mary Drone's life. In bitter fact, they brought her nothing but a constant state of financial anxiety. Witness:

John Drone drove the car to work every day, and Mary was left precisely as high and dry in Rolling Knolls as though John were still taking the bus. The vacuum cleaner, the dryer, the dishwasher and dispose-all made a mockery of Mary's housework, and left her with at least two more hours each day to enjoy the benefits of life in Rolling Knolls. Or, as Mr. Mendelsohn observes, the net effect of development wives' gadgets "gives the ladies more time to talk to other ladies with more time and what the hell do they do with this time? That's the problem."

The gadgets also give Mary more time to watch television tell her about more gadgets. Remember, Folly Gay's cake mix was predicated on the theory that it could be hurriedly made in order to be eaten as you watched television. It was a "taste treat for your TV supper," she said. A recent advertisement was even more blunt. It showed a family grouped around a glowing television set in the foreground, a washing machine spinning in the background. Your washing machine, the ad said, is working for you, washing and drying your clothes so you won't miss a minute at your television set—where, no doubt, the bemused family finds still other gadgets for sale.

There is no doubt many gadgets were purchased purely for prestige, the purchase motivated by that ageless habit, common among ineffectual people, of keeping up with the Joneses. Certainly John Drone's power mower was such a purchase. Drone, Lawrence Faint, Henry Amiable and Buster Fecund had, early in their acquaintance, contributed two dollars each toward a hand lawn mower with which to pare their tiny plots. Through the marvels of mass communication, and through desire to be one up on the folks next door, Fecund became aware of the power mower and bought one. Then Faint succumbed, then Amiable, and Drone was left sole owner, by default, of the push-me-pull-me.

"No use your killing yourself," Mary said coldly. "Everyone else has a power mower. You look ridiculous. We can afford one as well as they."

"We need a power mower like we need a third foot," Drone said. "I could cut all four lawns in fifteen minutes with the hand mower. Do you know how much those things cost?"

"You're sweaty and pale as a sheet," Mary said. "They cost five dollars down and a dollar a week at SOB Hardware."

Two days later, John Drone had his. Perhaps it was only right that, in trying to start the machine, he tangled the cord in the flywheel, didn't let go, and broke his wrist. He paid the doctor on time, too.

The gadget craze swept over America, and it is fitting that the last word should arrive from a development in Texas, where all events verge on the apocryphal. It seems there is a development of $85,000 houses, all alike, all built in a straight line on a plain near Dallas, each with its back-yard swimming pool. Two neighbors discussed an evil trick their builder had perpetrated.

"You'd think," said one, "that in a house like this, they'd give you a bigger deepfreeze."

"Yeah," his friend said, looking sourly at the frosted sepulcher that was identical to the one in his house. "Look at that. Just twenty stinking cubic feet."

It was in the field of home repairs that the hucksters out-did themselves, however. The need for repairs and physical improvements in the houses that Jerry had built across the nation was only too obvious. It was equally obvious that most development householders were young and hence could not afford to hire the necessary labor. Therefore, through TV and every other medium of mass communication, the young homeowners were reminded of their American heritage. In this land of the rugged pioneer, of Yankee ingenuity, that old knack called know-how was never lost. Therefore, the advertisers brayed, you, too, can do it yourself.

John Drone was only one of many thousands who swallowed this swill, never reflecting that ingenious Yankees came few to the hill, and that most log cabins were classic illustrations of leaky, draughty, substandard housing. Moreover, the John Drones of 1947–56 were 100 years removed from the aspects of desperate need that had turned their ancestors into rough carpenters. Many, especially those coming from cities to suburban developments, had never seen a miter box. But here, again, the communications media had an answer—simple plans, simple kits. Of course, a few tools would be necessary.

And so, in every shopping center in every development, the hardware store became the briskest money-maker, next to the supermarket. Some, like SOB Hardware, sold everything from tacks to prefabricated steel garages. Naturally, everything was sold on time, and if you didn't want to buy a hammer with your tacks, SOB could rent you one. It was somehow poetic that Mr. Burmal had opened his hardware store in the shopping center on the very day a high wind blew all the shingles off George Spleen's house. Mr. Burmal, ever the veteran's friend, was right on hand to help George buy the things George needed to repair the house Mr. Burmal had built for George.

In the normal course of do-it-yourself, Lawrence Faint discovered he'd have to purchase $785 worth of tools to assemble the packaged kit dollhouse he'd bought for his twin girls; Buster Fecund fell off his roof whilst replacing the corroding gutters; Drone put up a gravity-defying monstrosity when he tried to follow the simple plans for the outdoor fireplace Burmal sold him, and Mr. Voter power-sawed halfway through his arm before he finished that picket fence.

The surge of do-it-yourself is by no means ended. If there was any originality about the affair, it would be as valuable a creative force as making music, painting pictures, or—say —writing books. After all, the arts are practiced only by do-it-yourselfers. The trouble with development do-it-yourself is that it winds up in a sterile monotony. To be sure, construction of each brick fireplace added something unusual to the lives of the constructors at Rolling Knolls, but they all purchased the same plans and the same bricks, and the final effect was to reinforce the monotony of the development. The identical fireplaces remained as mocking monuments to the futility of mass escape.

Likewise, the women's aspect of do-it-yourself wound up in the same muck. Each Rolling Knolls home, decorated by a female do-it-yourselfer on advice from television, magazines and the Sunday papers, came in time to sport the same trivet on the wall, the same cardboard mobile, the same TV hassocks, the same plastic primitive bookends, the same drapes hung the same way. As noted, the ladies followed the fads in food purchases at the supermarket and it became—and remains—impossible to go to a party in Rolling Knolls and escape potato chips and clam dip.

While people with things to sell gave do-it-yourself its greatest impetus, many a project was dictated by need, and do-it-yourself reached its fullest flower with Mrs. Voter's project, the RK Pool. Frustrated by everyone's refusal to join in her back-yard improvement schemes, but still aware Rolling Knolls needed a community recreation area of some kind, Mrs. Voter was the prime mover in acquisition of a near-by bit of swamp as the site of a future community swimming pool.

"We'll divert the underground streams leading into the swamp and at the same time have a good head of water to supply the pool," she decreed, pulling odd bits of engineering misinformation together out of the air.

"If everybody pitches in to do the work, if we all do it ourselves, we'll have a pool in by next summer."

To buoy everyone's spirits for the arduous toils ahead,

Mrs. Voter had written a song. She passed around song sheets and led the singing. These are the words of the chorus; the reader will have to puzzle the tune out for himself:

So pack up your bathing suit
And jump right in
The R . . . K Pool.

Soon after the land had been purchased, it was discovered no underground streams fed the developing swamp in the low ground. The swamp was entirely fed by runoff from Rolling Knolls septic tanks, trickling across the clay hardpan not far below the surface.

Plans were thereupon changed, expensively. There would have to be a well. There would have to be sewer drains.

Meanwhile, few Rolling Knolls men came to help with the digging. It had been Mrs. Voter's plan that if every man dug a bit each day, there would be no need to hire a construction gang with its scoop shovels and drag buckets.

"Do you want to swim in the sweat of your neighbor's brow?" she asked John Drone point-blank. "I've done more work on this project than you have, John Drone, and my doctor says I need a rest. But you weren't down at the poolsite all week. We'll need the help of everyone if we're to do the job do you want your charter lifetime membership in the RK Pool or do you not?"

Idly, it occurred to Drone there was something very like the sound of doom in the words "lifetime membership." But he said he'd help, next day.

Alas, that day never arrived, for that very evening, a fist fight broke out at the meeting of the pool's board of directors over the suggeston that people from the neighboring developments, Valley View Dell, be invited to join the project and a contractor hired to finish the pool on the resultant proceeds of Valley View-ers' contributions.

In the end, Valley View Dell came in, the contractor was hired, and everyone was assessed another twenty-five dollars under threat of loss of his lifetime membership. The contractor didn't finish the pool in time for the first summer's use, and the second year health authorities ordered it closed because of an outbreak of polio, but the third summer amply demonstrated the pool's basic inability to minister to the needs of two big development populations.

Meanwhile, as the years passed for Mary Drone in her strange, futile milieu, she suspected life and youth were slipping away. Because she was not a thinking person, and enjoyed no point of vantage, she did not understand why the gadgets failed, why do-it-yourself failed, why TV bored her, why her neighbors (whom she called her friends) irritated her, why everything she did wound up in frustration. Naturally, it did not occur to her that the basic fault with her life was that she did not live in what sociologists call a community. Nor was she conscious that the passing years were slowly turning her from a rather placid, once pretty woman into a conventional nag.

One night in 1954, when John Drone came home as usual, parked the car in front as usual, and came up the walk as usual, Mary opened the door as usual, and—as had become usual—did not respond to the meaningless kiss.

"It's Tuesday," she said flatly, with ominous calm.

"I know," John said. "What's eating you?"

"It's Tuesday," Mary repeated. "On Tuesday evenings we go to the shopping center.

"And that's all we do. All day long I have to live in this horrid little house. The only thing I can ever do is stay right here, looking at the same things, until it's Tuesday.

"There is nothing," she said, still speaking in a flat, thin voice John Drone had never heard before, "that I can do to show that I am really Mary Drone. I haven't had a new dress for years. These clothes, if you'd like to know, are clothes I bought when I was in high school."

"What's the matter with that?" John asked puzzled. "You're lucky you can still wear them; they look fine. I bet you Gladys Fecund couldn't get into her last *year's* clothes."

"For God's sake!" Mary said, her voice beginning to break. "Even if we could afford new clothes, we couldn't afford to go anywhere if there was anywhere to go. I wonder and wonder why we're living at all—these are supposed to be the happiest years of my life."

With that she broke from him, ran to their bedroom and, for the first time in their married life, locked the door.

"What's the matter with Mommy?" Chip wanted to know.

"It beats me," said a shaken John Drone.

"You made Mommy cry," Kim explained.

Dinner that evening was a tense affair, and after the children had gone to bed, John and Mary Drone sat down to talk about themselves rather than drive to the shopping center.

"If you carry on this way, you'll wind up with Dr. Sly," John said, referring to Dr. Sigmund F. Sly, the youthful psychiatrist who'd had the foresight to open a residential office in Rolling Knolls. He was just a few doors away, on Kasserine Pass.

It is to John and Mary's credit that their discussion led them to conclude Mary needed something to do she could call her own. The great difficulty, however, was that Mary didn't know what she wanted to do, and was unwilling to attempt something she'd never done before. Perhaps this was because Mary's personality was not basically strong, or perhaps it was the result of her conditioning since infancy. Before she left home to go to school, Mary's mother had told her what to do. At school, teachers had told her what to do. In Mary's married life, magazines, Sunday papers, radio, TV and the constant company of her exact equals in Rolling Knolls had told her what to do. In John Drone, she'd married her equal, so perhaps it was John's conditioning that had led him to suggest, however facetiously, Dr. Sly, for development people believe that when one doesn't know what to do, **one** goes to someone who can always tell them what to do.

"There's nothing very wrong with you," Dr. Sly told Mary the following morning. "You're just bored. You think your life is monotonous. It is. My life is too monotonous, too, listening to women tell me the same stories every day. Everybody's life is monotonous; your case isn't unusual.

"What you need," Dr. Sly said, "is to get out of the house more often. Let your husband baby-sit and take yourself a vacation a couple of nights a week. Go window-shopping—go to the movies. Or, have you considered a hobby? How would you like to do some ceramics? There is a group of women right here in Rolling Knolls organized into a ceramics class. They're over on Guadalcanal Drive. Why not go and see how you like it?"

Mary went. And Mary's ash trays didn't look a whit better than any other woman's ash trays. In fact, they didn't take a glaze as well. After a few feeble efforts at the potter's art, Mary realized it was not for her. Moreover, the conversation of the ceramics class was as near the breaking point as a falling Ming vase, for each woman felt the need to discuss her personal problems, to burden her classmates with her private difficulties, and each woman had the same problems. Problems that were, of course, Mary's as well, for each woman had come to the ceramics class for the same reason. After two weeks, Mary gave it up.

Opportunely enough, Gladys Fecund provided as good an answer to Mary Drone's galloping ennui as anything Rolling Knolls could ever offer.

"You know what Eve Wild and I have been doing?" she asked Mary one morning.

"No, what?"

"Well, you know Eve," Gladys said. "Almost nobody's ever been in her house, because she has never asked anybody in. Those friends of theirs, I don't know who they are, all come from the city.

"Well, I was just determined I was going to find out what Eve Wild's house was like, so I went over the other evening and knocked, and there was Eve, with a painter's smock on.

" 'Oh, have you been painting?' I said. 'I didn't know you were an artist, Eve, can I see what you're doing?'

"Of course Eve had to say 'yes,' and my stars! You've no idea! Eve is the most . . . Why she does beautiful things, simply beautiful. Such colors! Why, the things she's done in that house, and the way she's fixed it up . . .

"Anyway," said Gladys smugly, "I told Eve it was mean to keep all that talent to herself, and would she show me how to do these things. So I've been at Eve's, painting! I asked if I could bring a friend, and Eve said 'Who?' and when I said you, Eve said, 'Oh, all right,' so can you come tonight to Eve's house with me?"

Everything about the Wilds' house fascinated Mary Drone, and at the same time made her a bit uneasy. Those strange, intelligent children, Abel and Delilah, seemed to regard Mary with a piercing compassion that was completely unnerving. An aura of self-sufficiency enfolded the family; the colors and furnishings of the Wild house made it difficult for Mary to believe she was in a Rolling Knolls home.

For two nights a week for several weeks the three women met at Eve's house, and under Eve's deft guidance, Mary's life began to take on hues she'd never suspected.

The first thing, Eve said, was to observe. Look at that lamp; see its light and dark areas? See how many subtle differences there are in the shadows? Now try to draw it . . . draw lightly . . . no, don't erase, just forget about that bad line for a while and work around the whole picture; the line that looks wrong now may have a use later on.

And for the first time, Mary began to observe, to think, to work really hard, to create, and then . . .

"Maryann Faint was wondering what we were doing, Eve," Gladys said one night. "And I told her about our arts-and-crafts study group. Maryann said she wished she could come, but I told her it was up to you."

There was no way out. Maryann came. And after Maryann came Jane Amiable, who said she wasn't any good at art at all, but she'd brought some mending with her—mending she'd meant to do for some time.

Then Jane wouldn't take no for an answer, the next meeting would have to be at her house, and Jane served coffee and cakes and introduced the ladies to a friend Jane had made on Kasserine Pass; another lady with collars to turn, socks to mend.

In less time than it takes to tell, what had begun as an amateur art group dedicated to personal salvation became a traveling, mending kaffeeklatsch, and nobody noticed when Eve withdrew, pleading the press of other business. It was another victory for the *élan vital* of Rolling Knolls, which is a leveling influence beside which a bulldozer seems like a baby's rattle. The immediate result was that Mary Drone mended and listened to further researches into child care, husbands and television shows until she, too, withdrew, defeated, to her life at home. She never drew another line.

The group didn't notice Mary's leaving, for there was something new to talk about in Rolling Knolls. The Wilds were moving!

Eve hadn't told a soul, but they'd sold their house and they were moving out and nobody knew why and nobody knew where. Everybody had always thought the Wilds were the only folks who liked Rolling Knolls. But Maryann Faint said she'd always thought the Wilds were kind of peculiar and in many ways it was a good riddance. Mrs. Voter put the Wilds' case, as she called it, on an intellectual plane. She said the Wilds were the kind of people who had no place in a well-integrated community.

Meanwhile, time, which might seem to stand forever still in a housing development, somehow passed nonetheless. The dwellers who had once been twenty-four years old became thirty-two. Their children, toilet-trained at last, edged toward the abyss of adolescence. Time played its little jokes, and something infinitely more serious than a new fad flickered through the boxlike houses of Rolling Knolls. Once again, because a housing development is an homogenous community, it seemed a case of spontaneous combustion.

Something infinitely more serious than a new fad.

Mary and John Drone were playing bridge with the Amiables one night, playing men against women as they'd done at least once a week for eight years. But this night, Mary became aware of the insistant pressure of Henry's knee. She edged away, but Henry's knee followed. There was no mistake. Things came into even sharper focus when, later in the evening, Jane got up to prepare a snack in the kitchen and John Drone very nearly upset the table in his rush to help her. For the first time, it occurred to Mary that John had always helped Jane recently. Henry's knee was accompanied this time by his hand.

"That's one good thing about the kitchens in our houses," he said softly, his myopic blue eyes strangely gleaming, "there's no doors on our kitchens."

And with that, he squeezed Mary's thigh.

"Henry," she said. "Please."

"I can't help it," he said. "I wouldn't be honest if I didn't say I want you. I've just realized I've been in love with you for years." Then, leaning back, removing his hand, he grinned at Mary and said as though it were all a joke. "In a purely platonic way, of course."

He laughed a laugh that was intended to deceive no one, and Mary looked with dismay into Henry's boiled blue eyes.

"Hey!" Henry called, winking at Mary, "you guys making love out there?"

John and Jane promptly reappeared, bringing cakes and coffee. It seemed to Mary they had reappeared a little too soon after Henry's call.

Now as everyone is well aware, temptations of the flesh have tugged at every breast since Lucifer's shabby victory in Eden, and, as Dr. Kinsey has pointed out, a certain number of men and women have succumbed to those temptations, particularly after the first decade of married life—particularly in certain social classes. A housing development like Rolling Knolls is nothing if not an entire sample class, ready-made for Dr. Kinsey's notebook, and ready-made for Lucifer as well.

In Rolling Knolls there were 498 young couples. Every summer evening for eight yeàrs, 498 young men in shorts and T shirts enjoyed the spectacle of 498 young ladies in shorts and halters, and for each of the 498 young men, there was always the pleasant speculation as to the talents, abilities and special qualities of 497 of those 498 young women they viewed. Proximity in this case constantly whetted the edge of speculation. And, as the years passed, the speculation in many cases became the wish, and the wish became the attempt.

Surely, enough has been written about sex in this country so that we don't have to belabor the matter here, but a few things may be said about the special aspects of sexual relationships in housing developments.

First, of course, there's the futility of playing interchangeable wives. It's futile on any moral ground, and it's even more futile on purely amoral grounds, for since everyone in a place like Rolling Knolls is almost exactly like everyone else in that place, you'd think it would surely occur to people like Henry Amiable there would be no difference in response between his wife and Mary Drone.

The devil of it is, this latter thought *did* occur to Henry Amiable, and the conscious expression of his thought was completely bizarre. It was manifested in the kind of party games that had begun to grow up after the block party had gone down to dusty death, and after television and other influences had brought about after-supper entertainment in groups of six and eight. Henry Amiable suggested a game which became wildly popular:

The men would go out of the living room into the kitchen, and the ladies would lie down on the living room floor, covering themselves with sheets. Then the men would come in, and try to guess whose wife was whose by a process resembling the reading of Braille type.

Gladys Fecund thought up the switch, of course. The ladies would be blindfolded, and grovel around on the living room floor, feeling the bared calves of the men, and try to guess whose husband was whose.

At one party of recent memory—a cocktail party which broke up into two separate groups of men and women—five women were observed trying on one another's wedding rings. It scarcely need be said that all the rings fitted all the women.

Such pastimes as these, such eloquent betrayals of the real thoughts of the players, reached their apotheosis in the annual masquerade party Mrs. Voter had got in the habit of giving each New Year's Eve. On the most recent occasion, the living room furniture was piled in the bedrooms, for Mrs. Voter had invited ten couples, including Dr. and Mrs. Sigmund F. Sly.

To the utter fascination of everyone, retiring Maryann Faint, the last person you'd ever suspect, came wearing gold paint, and not another thing. She was a statue, she said, and in no time both men and women were touching her "to see if you're solid gold." Buster Fecund came as a satyr, of course, wearing a pair of goatskin breeches, sporting a tiny tail and little horns. There was a man from Kasserine Pass who came as a minstrel, and his wife came in a negligee, carrying a sign reading THINK. To those who could not think, she confessed she was the "Lay of the Last Minstrel." But it remained for Dr. Sly and his wife to turn up in formal evening clothes, making their excuses.

"When we said we'd come," he explained to the sallow,

bony cancan dancer who was Mrs. Voter, "we had completely forgotten we had this other party, but we didn't want to miss yours. So we went to the other party first, and there wasn't time to change, so we came as we were."

He smiled, and made a charming little gesture. There wasn't a word of truth in his excuse.

It is a matter of sober fact that the next working day, a Monday, Dr. Sly called up a colleague and made an appointment to find out why he'd been afraid to attend a masquerade party in costume.

The pressure of the dirty jokes at the cocktail parties, the pressure of the prurient games, the pressure of Henry Amiable's knee, all left Mary Drone slightly seasick, and it was a sickness for which there was no relief, for the jokes, the games and Henry's innuendoes went on and on and there was no escape.

But more people than Mary Drone were seasick in the pitching lifeboat that was Rolling Knolls, for the fact of the matter is that the growing lusts were not curbed, and they found no outlet. Rolling Knolls was far too intimate a place in which to conduct an affair, and everyone knew it only too well. Lacking Dr. Kinsey's time, organization, knowledge and special methods, and refusing to accept hearsay evidence, the kindest conclusion that will be drawn here is that such pangs as beset Henry Amiable raged on, unassuaged—at least unassuaged in Rolling Knolls.

Moreover, the atmosphere of brooding sexual anxiety and frustration lurking over the thirty-two to thirty-eight-year-olds of Rolling Knolls was accentuated by the fact it was a common problem. All hands were aware of it, even as they went on with their giddy games. Further, this atmosphere was deepened for everyone, every day, through the resources of TV, radio, movies, newspapers and magazines, for a bulk of the stories dwelt continually on sexual love, and the advertisements were (and are) almost entirely predicated on dreams of sexual conquest. A girdle merchant suggests to you, madame, that his product will result in your luring to your bed the handsome knight of your yearnings, and the automobile merchant suggests to you, sir, that the big-breasted houri poised by the gleaming open door of his newest model comes with the heap. Mr. Philip Wylie has dealt extensively with this aspect of American culture in his excellent *Generation of Vipers,* so the only point we'll make here is that all Rolling Knolls families are the special prey of all means of mass communication, and that, en masse, they absorb the full dose of the sexual preoccupation of our times.

As the discerning reader might by now suspect, Mary Drone wasn't enjoying a rousing good time in Rolling Knolls. In fact, she was fed to the teeth, and it eventually dawned upon her to follow the Wilds' example and clear out. From our point of omniscience, we can see Mary had no real friends in Rolling Knolls—she merely had acquaintances who forced her to become involved in their emotional problems. She had no conceivable interest in her house, no means of escape from the crushing sameness of development life. The work-saving gadgets brought her no real reward and mass-communicated fads did not enlarge her happiness, but simply indicated the level of her boredom by her willingness to accept them. Finally, the development was becoming a steamy culture of social sickness. None of these reasons for her frustration were apparent to Mary, however. She put her finger on another reason, that most readily obvious—the family needed more space.

Chip was eleven, Kim, seven, and the children took up all the space there was on the living room floor when they sprawled out to do their homework. There was literally no space to walk around them. The children needed space to play. They'd outgrown the apparatus in the cluttered back yard; the swings stood unused for months at a time. Normally, Chip should be playing those games that take up great fields—games like baseball and football. Neither game could be played in Rolling Knolls. Certainly they could not be played in the tiny, fenced yards. And no one wanted the kids to play in the streets—too many automobiles already bore evidence of sharply-struck baseballs.

Penning an eleven-year-old boy into a fenced back yard the size of a cemetery plot is as difficult as stuffing a Great Dane into a cat basket, and every bit as reasonable an operation. There was no question about it, Chip needed space—lots of it. And Kim needed space as well. For too long now, Mary had worried about the children's advancing years—they badly needed separate bedrooms. Mary, of course, needed space in every sense, but she was thinking purely of space in the physical sense when she told John Drone one spring day of 1956 that they'd have to move.

"There's no getting around it, we need three bedrooms," she said.

"Maybe I can build another room on the house," John said. "How about finishing up the attic into a dormitory for the kids?"

"Chip's nearly as tall as I am," Mary said icily, "and I can't stand up straight in that attic. Besides, have you ever poked your head up there in the summer? And where do you think we're going to put all the things we've stored in the attic if we make it into a bedroom?

"Besides," she said, "the children don't want a dormitory. What they need are separate bedrooms."

"Well, what do you want me to do about it?" John asked.

"Buy a larger house," Mary said, as though to a child.

"But we haven't finished paying for this one."

"We don't have to. I saw in the paper yesterday where people are trading their old houses in on larger houses. It's no different from trading an old car on a new car. Your old house in down payment on a new house—it's as simple as that," Mary said.

"You have any place in mind, for instance?"

"I've been looking at the ads for a new split-level house in Maryland," Mary said, going through the evening paper. "It says there are four bedrooms, maid's room, two baths, maid's bath, cathedral ceilings, floor to ceiling walls, two living rooms, a study, spacious dining area, modern kitchen with built-in birch cabinets, and all for nothing down."

"What do you have to pay besides nothing down?" John wondered.

"Nothing," Mary said. "It says here no settlement charges —nothing down at all, and a thirty-year mortgage. All for only $16,970."

"WHAT?"

"Sixteen thousand dollars," Mary said.

"Does it say what the monthly charges are, with nothing down?"

"No," Mary said.

"They're probably scared to print them," John muttered. Over the years, as his credit rating had improved, John had learned slowly and painfully.

"If people couldn't afford them, they wouldn't sell them," Mary explained. "Anyway, it won't hurt us a bit to look. And

I might as well tell you now, we're going to have to move, so we are just going to have to start looking."

"Where is this place, again?"

"In Montgomery County."

"Do you realize that's the highest-tax county in the whole Washington area?"

"But the taxes are in the mortgage payments, aren't they?" Mary persisted. "Anyway, we'll only be looking."

"What's the name of this place?"

"Hardwood Forest," Mary said. "You go out Georgia Avenue, past Silver Spring, past Wheaton, past Glenmont, near Olney."

"Olney," John said. "Olney is just thirty miles from town."

Drone was a long time getting to sleep that night. He had almost finished paying for the car. They now owned the television set and the dryer. In a year or so, they might begin to save money.

And now Mary wanted to start all over.

What was wrong with her, anyway?

5. It's Only Money

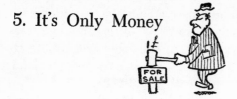

"Easy come, easy go."—Old American folk saying

A SERIES of roadside signs prepared John and Mary Drone for the wonders of Hardwood Forest. There were dozens of them, spaced along the highway like Burma Shave signs: "SPLIT LEVELS—Four Bedrooms—Maid's Room—Two Baths—Study—Maid's Bath—Dining Room—TWO living rooms—Servant's Entrance—Floor to Ceiling Walls—$16,970—NOTHING DOWN—JUST AHEAD."

And then came a huge sign of a nearly-naked drum majorette who, apparently, was in love with "Tri-Level Living" and wanted YOU to try it.

Once past the dancing soubrette, the Drones found a gaudy Maryland state flag snapping in the sun of the new day, and running down from the flagstaff were gay little varicolored pennants. The Drones parked in the "visitors' parking area" and contemplated a row of sample houses. Each house was different, and each bore a name. There was the Riviera with its "cathedral ceiling" (a steep roof); the Acapulco with its mission tile; the Monte Carlo with the tremendous glass wall; the Beachcomber with its tiny flagstone terrace. And behind these samples there rolled away as far as the eye could see an undulating red-clay plain studded with replicas of the sample houses, and beyond the rows and rows of houses, out on the horizon's rim, bulldozers were obliterating the last of the slash pines that had once covered the land.

The Drones beheld this with conditioned eyes. After nearly ten years in the Washington metropolitan area, they regarded the scene as completely normal. Progress was under way—man was once again bringing order and beauty out of Nature's mad chaos, offering a helping hand to God, as it were.

"Come right in," the salesman intoned as the Drones came up the walk to pause before the first house, the Riviera. "Welcome to Hardwood Forest's homes of tomorrow."

He was completely unlike any salesman the Drones had met before. He was tall, his dark hair edged with gray at the temples, dressed in sober garb, his black shoes brightly polished. He could have been, and probably had been, a crackerjack undertaker's assistant.

"My name is Roland Suave," he said. "I'm here to answer any questions you might have."

"There are four bedrooms?" Mary asked.

"Let me show you through the house," Mr. Suave said. "This, you see, is the living room. And the dining area is nine by ten feet."

"I thought your signs said 'dining room,'" Drone said.

"Quite right," Mr. Suave agreed. "In the Riviera, there is *room* to dine. We offer more dining space than any home in this price bracket. You would have to pay at least $23,000 for any four-bedroom house in the Washington area that had a separate dining room."

He smiled a bit superciliously.

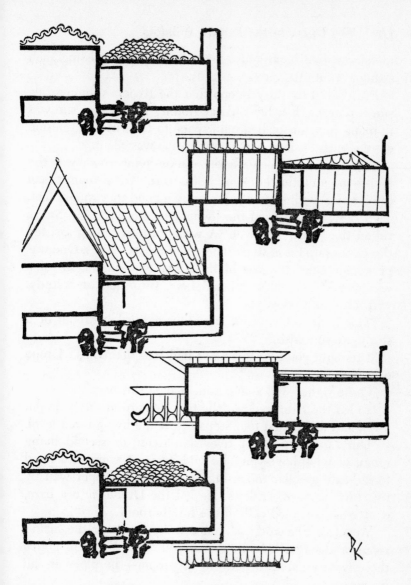

There were four sample houses.

"That would be an older house," he said, dismissing such a thought into the outer darkness.

It occurred to Mary Drone that the Riviera's dining area was no larger than her own at Rolling Knolls, but she was thinking in terms of bedroom space to the virtual exclusion of all else these days, and therefore she was silent.

On the same level with the dining-living room was the bathroom and the kitchen. Both were larger rooms than the Drones' Rolling Knolls house by a good four square feet. Two steps led up from the living room to what Mr. Suave called the "bedroom level." A wrought-iron railing assisted the Drones up those steps. There were three rooms. One was perhaps a third the size of the other two, with a slit of a window. This monk's cell had been furnished as a study, with desk and bookcase.

"This," Mr. Suave said, "is either a third bedroom or a study, as you wish."

"I thought you said this place had four bedrooms," Drone objected.

"Quite right," Mr. Suave said. "Come this way."

He led the Drones down the two steps from the bedroom level, and descended four steps below the living room level.

"Our family room, or television room, or second living room, or what-have-you," he said, waving a graceful hand to indicate a cellar room, faintly lit near its upper wall by two tiny, narrow windows. He led the Drones into a bare, cinder-block-walled cell off the family room.

"And this," he said, "as you can see, is either the maid's room or the fourth bedroom, as you wish. You will notice there is an unfinished bath off this room—the pipes are all in place."

A cellar door opened directly into the unfinished bedroom.

Mary, who was beginning to understand Hardwood Forest's signs and language at last, correctly guessed this was the "Servant's Entrance." There was a film of moisture seeping under the door and spreading slowly on the bare concrete floor.

"All this," Mr. Suave said with delighted surprise, "is only $20,000! If you wish us to go ahead and floor and finish the fourth bedroom and install the bath, we can do it for an extra $2450."

"Twenty-two thousand dollars!" John Drone exclaimed. "I thought your signs said $16,970."

"This is the Riviera," Mr. Suave explained patiently. "The Acapulco, next door, is only $19,980; the Monte Carlo is $18,885—you must be referring to the, ah, Beachcomber. Unfortunately," he said, looking at his nails, "there are no Beachcombers left. They were our most popular model . . . three bedrooms, maid's room, study, two baths, genuine four-by-five-foot flagstone patio . . ."

"You mean two bedrooms and a room you could use for either a bedroom or a maid's room or a study, and a place for a bath later on," Mary corrected him.

"Exactly!" Mr. Suave agreed. "Anything you wish. I see you see the adaptability of a Hardwood Forest Home of Tomorrow. Adaptability to meet the growing family need! Mr. Tony Lightheart, the builder, studied good building design for several years in Hollywood, and was one of the first men in the country completely to understand the special advantages one finds in tri-level living. Split levels," he confided, "are sweeping the nation."

"A split level looks to me," John said dubiously, "like you just dug half a basement half deep enough and finished it off and stuck the bedrooms over the basement room."

Mr. Suave regarded John coldly.

"How much, may I ask, do you earn?" he asked.

"Let's put it this way; how much do I have to pay a month for this house with nothing down?"

"If you are a veteran and have not used your GI eligibility for a guaranteed loan, you may, of course, purchase a Riviera home here for nothing down," Mr. Suave said. "But in that case, we would have to be satisfied you were earning at least ten thousand dollars a year with a reputable concern.

"Taxes," Mr. Suave said distastefully, "are $270; utilities, $30; insurance, $90—all approximately, of course—and your monthly payments under a thirty-year-mortgage would be somewhere in the neighborhood of, ah, $150. At the very, very least."

"Suppose we could put out $3000 down," John suggested.

"In that case, your monthly payments would be about, oh, say, $115," Mr. Suave guessed, "but we would have to be sure you were earning at least $7500 a year."

"Ha," Mary said.

"May I show you the Acapulco, or the Monte Carlo?" Mr. Suave asked. "There are a few left."

"No thanks," John said.

"I am very sorry," Mr. Suave said sincerely. "We should have liked to have had you at Hardwood Forest."

On the long trip back to Rolling Knolls, John and Mary Drone realized they'd have to do extensive househunting if they were to add a third bedroom to their lives without more than doubling their present monthly mortgage payments. The fact that Hardwood Forest in topography, number of trees, layout, monotony and remoteness from schools, recreational areas and shopping centers was precisely as disadvantageous as Rolling Knolls never once entered their minds. They thought only of bedroom space. Mary, in fact, had rather liked the Riviera.

But the money . . . the money.

They talked it over that evening, going over the familiar family books. The account ledgers reflected the Drones' life, and this is the story they told:

As pencil procurement officer for the Census Bureau's Division of Miscellaneous Statistics, John Drone earned $5500 a year. When he'd first moved into Rolling Knolls, he had not earned that much, but then, his costs had been less. His taxes, for example, went from $100 to $185 in that eight-year period; water-rent and trash-collection costs rose from $30 to $70. As county needs increased, special assessments grew. This, in 1956, was Drone's annual budget:

State and county taxes, $185; house repair and maintenance, $70; water and trash services, $70; gas and hot water, $200; electricity, $80; telephone (remember he was a suburban resident), $80; food and milk, $1385; payments on time-purchased clothing and household gadgets, $660; mortgage payments (principal and interest), $780; upkeep, gas and oil for car, $600; insurance (including medical), $132; newspaper, $21; recreation (at $13 a month), $156.

This left a rousing $1081, at which point Uncle Sam stepped up for his cut—about $500—and the Drones were left with $581—about $12 a week—to fritter away on such trivia as doctors' bills, medicine, magazines, vacations, soap, toilet paper, cosmetics, cigarets, shoelaces, nail clippers, birthdays and Christmas.

Naturally, the Drones had no savings account. They had long ago spent the $300 worth of war bonds their parents had given them for a wedding present. They'd never been able to take a vacation any gaudier than a weekend at

Chesapeake Bay's jellyfish-infested shoreline. Their checking account was maintained by a balancing act that would have made a slack-wire artist green with envy. Their equity in their box at Rolling Knolls was almost exactly $3000—in nearly half the mortgage term they had paid off not quite one-third the principal. All in all, the state of the Drones' finances made for an interesting problem, and the solution to this problem wasn't made a bit easier by Mary's demand that they buy an even larger house, at an even larger, longer mortgage.

You might even think they couldn't afford to move.

. . . there lay Hope gleaming faintly . . .

Still, it must be remembered that when all the woes and torments stormed forth from Pandora's box, there lay Hope gleaming faintly in the bottom of the empty chest. Like millions of other development dwellers, John and Mary Drone adopted Hope as their very own child. To them, to hope was to feel certain.

Surely the lynx-eyed reader will have noticed that Drone's financial health was predicated on the theory that he would never lose his job or have to take a salary cut or suffer catastrophic illness. For that matter, his fiscal affairs hung in such balance that no one in the family could afford to come down with expensive dental complaints or any sickness costing more than twenty dollars' worth of today's scatter-shot antibiotics. If anyone in the clan had died, there wouldn't have been enough ready cash to bury him in the cheapest plot without a coffin. But the Drones paid all this no-never-mind; they simply hoped none of these things would take place. They sailed as rapidly as possible across the vastest of oceans in a tissue-paper boat, hoping to get to shore before the hull soaked through, hoping there'd never be a storm. And in this, they had only too much company. Times, customs and attitudes have changed. In these years, the John Drones of our developments need no hope but hope itself.

There used to be an era—oh, so long ago—when an article was offered for sale at one price. There used to be a general feeling that if a thing cost more than you could afford, you did without. Or, if a thing could not be bought today, you saved your pennies in order to buy it tomorrow. But these quaint notions are as dead as Benjamin Franklin, for an entire generation has grown up to imitate in private lives the zany government philosophy of deficit finance that has prevailed since the 1930's. Easy credit is the diseased heart of our prosperity, and today a whole nation is involved in opening its Christmas presents two weeks before Thanksgiving.

Costs too much? But you want it, don't you? Well, why not go ahead and buy it anyway? Why not pay as you use, and buy it on time? Why not, indeed?

These days, not only are cars and expensive gadgets sold on time, but also clothes and—God save us all—vacations. You buy your time on time. All that is lacking is a national food-sales campaign advising us to eat now, pay later. Children of their times, the nations' development dwellers would not find this idea in the least unusual, for development people are our chiefest consumers of time-bought goods. Moneylenders know our Drones well. Cheerfully, they loan Drone more and more and more to meet his mounting debts and see no evil in what they do. The fact, however, is that six million American families are currently delinquent in their installment payments.

Toward harvest time of 1955, both a major news service and the Scripps-Howard newspaper chain looked into this state of things, and what they saw gave them the heebie-jeebies. It was immediately apparent to both organizations that development dwellers constitute a vast slice of the consumer public, and that financial overextension was a fundamental part of development life. Therefore, both examined development-family finances from coast to coast, and served up the resultant statistics in the form of a sample family's plight.

The news syndicate story's sample family, a New Jersey lot, took home $72.25 a week and spent all but $7.61 of it each week on taxes, mortgage, food, utilities, telephone, insurance, hospitalization, payment on a bank note and union dues. That $7.61 left over had to provide clothing, recreation and upkeep of the family car. This was a family of four living in an $11,500 box on a slab, and they purchased—on time—a $170 record player, a $139 television set, a $319 deepfreeze and an $800 automobile. Naturally, the family has many times gone to a bank to ask for small loans, and at the time of writing, there was a $450 note coming due. They'd borrowed that to pay their debts. Since they paid their debts, their credit rating was A-1 with the merchants. Since they'd somehow repaid their three previous bank notes, their credit rating was A-1 with the bank. But most illuminating were the quoted remarks of the man of this shaky house:

"Most of the young people we know are buying everything on time," the sample householder said. "Most of them have four or five bills coming in every month for things they've bought on time. A lot of them have a new car every year. They get anything they want.

"I guess they can afford it better than we can. Most of the people we know, the husband and wife both work and a lot of the men hold down two jobs—a regular day job and then a part-time night job. They do all right . . .

"It's only the older people who talk about a depression. My father-in-law is always talking about the danger of another depression and warning us we'd better save our money and be careful. He talks about what happened in the big depression. But Helen and I were only about 10 years old then. We don't remember about it. If you don't remember something like that—I guess you just don't worry about it."

This family, like the Drones, also lived in belief there would be no hard luck, no catastrophic illness.

The syndicate's feature story went on to say that consumer credit was (in the last quarter of 1955) already $32 billion and rising fast; that the nation's mortgage debt was $82 billion and rising faster. The story said Federal Reserve System officials were somewhat perplexed by all this—they didn't know whether the situation was good or bad; couldn't make up their minds whether Americans should spend money they didn't have for things they might not need.

Federal Reserve figures showed the total of $114 billion in consumer and mortgage debts was less than half the nation's income after taxes—and government feeling was that this situation was perfectly sound *as long as employment kept up to record peaks.*

Moreover, the story pointed out, government planners were scared to blow the whistle on easy credit, for this might mean a slowdown in sales. Auto sales, for example. Sales slowdowns mean layoffs in factories, which mean jobless voters, which mean exactly what you think it means— depression and political belching. Hence, Washington's planners today speak glibly of "a healthy inflation."

The Scripps-Howard newspapers' sample family lived with their five children in a Cape Cod development house, also costing $11,500 (and where they put the kids is something the story never said), and the family earned $5700 a year, presumably after taxes. The family therefore took in $475 a month and spent $438, leaving about $9 a week to spend on gifts, holidays, school expenses, auto upkeep, sundries and household maintenance. Once again, no provision was made for loss of job, cut in pay or unexpected medical bills. Instead, this sample family was also up to here in hock and it, too, had worn a rut between its mortgaged manor and the bank, constantly hiring money to meet the time payments on the car, the aluminum storm windows, the $300 television set, the expensive washer and other gadgets of our time.

All this gave rise to a Scripps-Howard editorial correctly appraising the situation from New York to California. Of their sample man, the newspapers said:

"His design is to live comfortably on ice as thin as his next week's pay check; in constant hock, with little or no cash, everything depending on tomorrow being just as good as today.

"For many, it would be a design for nightmare.

"But the pattern for life of millions of Americans is just like that . . ."

Such people, the editorial said, "apparently haven't the judgment to see the possible disaster lurking in the nothing-down-and-a-dollar-forever debt, if you pile it up too high. They'd be stony in a week if they lost their jobs or were hit by catastrophic illness. But there is no reason those who control credit have to be equally reckless."

While the newspaper organizations were primarily interested in issuing a public warning, others are more interested in the effect of an easy-credit philosophy on the development dwellers themselves. American University's Harold Mendelsohn has considered the situation for some time.

"The frightening thing," he said, "is that these people have no discipline. They are spending all their salaries, every week. Buying gadgets is often a form of recreation for them, or they buy gadgets to make their homes more bearable. And, incidentally, none of them own their homes."

Mr. Mendelsohn explained that, from a sociologist's point of view, ownership of a house implies a certain financial stability. The householder must actually have responsible equity in his property.

"All these people have in their houses is psychological ownership," he said. "They sit down with a real-estate man and pay nothing down, but pass papers back and forth over a desk. The papers say the purchaser has the right to live in the house as long as he pays sixty-five dollars a month every month for thirty years. Miss out on those sixty-five-dollar payments, and woosh, he's out. He's not only out of the house but he still has to pay the debt. Going into bankruptcy won't wipe out the debt, as many veterans are now discovering. Maybe they thought the government guarantee on the mortgage was a kind of gift to them. All it means is the government pays the bank the guaranteed amount, and the government then tries to collect this sum from the veteran while the bank tries to recover the balance from him.

"Meanwhile, a development householder these days can come home in his unpaid-for car, mow the lawn with his not-yet-bought power mower, sit in his mortgaged house, turn on the encumbered television set and say to himself, 'I am prosperous Joe Doakes. Everywhere I look I see that which is mine.' Such a man is living in a fool's paradise."

Appropriately enough, the fools living in this nothing-down paradise have no idea what they should pay for anything they buy. There is no way they can tell what anything really costs—if there is today such a thing as the "real" cost. In Hagerstown, Maryland, for example, a filling-station proprietor was allowed $850 for his 1950 car plus a $600 reduction in the price of a new $3900 car. His helper bought the 1950 car back for $350—$25 down and two years to pay the rest. In other words, the new-car dealer blithely chopped the price of his $3900 model by $1100 just like that, without turning a hair. Presumably, the auto dealer is not a philanthropist and must make a profit to stay in business. What then was the real price of that $3900 car? Just try to find out.

Likewise, the prices of electrical appliances are all over the lot. One Philadelphian went to an appliance dealer to price air conditioners. He was told the model he wanted cost $495. It is a matter of stony fact he bought that conditioner for $270, installed, simply by protesting $495 was more than he wanted to pay. General Motors told a vast television audience they have so priced their appliances that dealers have enough spread to be able to offer good trade-ins for old appliances and generous terms for the balance, using the old appliance as down payment.

So how much do these things cost? Nobody—no consumer —really knows. They are, however, told all the time by mass-communications advertising, and by one another, that they really need, really can't afford to be without, rotating chicken toasters, electrical blankets, aluminum storm windows, deepfreeze chests, bigger television sets remotely controlled, dishwashing machines, cars you drive by pushing buttons and high-fidelity radios on which to catch the purest tones of the current commercial.

And what do such gadgets actually add to the lives of their purchasers? It is possible to roast a chicken without an electrical spit, to keep warm without an electrical blanket; the increased furnace bill is by no means as great—even over a period of twenty years—as the cost of those storm windows; frozen food costs thirty per cent more per edible pound than nonfrozen food; the same sad programs look no better on a larger screen; it is still possible to wash dishes by hand and remain alive; a gear-shift car provides cheaper transportation than a car with an automatic transmission and it gets you there just as fast; no amount of high-fidelity listening will ever be as valuable a human experience as personal attendance—just once—at the concert hall.

Even if our development dwellers are aware of these matters, the fact remains they buy gadgets, expensive gadgets, on time and in great quantity. They will skimp on the family food and clothing budget to buy them. In short, they buy things they could do without at a price they cannot afford, and they know not what they're buying, nor stop to wonder why, and they haven't the vaguest clue as to what these things really cost. Nor, for that matter, do they understand what those gadgets really do—to them.

As with gadgets, so with houses. Indeed, today's development house is apt to be sold on the basis of the gadgets it contains, rather than on its ability to answer the real human needs of its inhabitants. Today's signs read "SPLIT LEVELS," and then, in type nearly as large, there will appear the name of the manufacturer of the kitchen gadgets the house contains. It is difficult for the purchaser of such a house to discover how much of his mortgage money is going into the purchase of those kitchen gadgets—contraptions whose retail price is wildly suspect. It is altogether possible, and indeed probable, that if the purchaser had been able to buy just the house, and supply his own identical gadgets purchased through some discount house, he could save himself several hundred dollars.

Even more at a loss than anyone else in this land to discover the true cost of things must have been the purchasers of those "completely equipped" development houses in Oklahoma. To pep up sales, the developer promised to pay the family's moving costs. He stuck a new car in the garage in case the family lacked a car, and threw in a live, kicking, Shetland pony for the kids. Nothing down, of course. The story may be apocryphal, but it's going the rounds and is retold here solely to illustrate that a point has been reached in our national life where such a story could possibly have some meaning. As a nation, we're ready to believe it, for we've lost all sight of fusty old Franklin's careful perspectives.

It is only against this Through The Looking Glass background that we can see how John and Mary Drone could conceivably think of moving into a larger house. Surely, some echo of Elm Street in Mary's mind must have told her it was impossible, but it is typical of today's frame of mind that she felt sure she and John could swing it, somehow. It is also typical of the nation's general attitude that the Drones never once considered anything but the purchase of a *new* house. Not for an instant did either entertain the notion of a spacious—and far cheaper—older house in city or country. To them, an older house would be a secondhand house, as odious as a secondhand car. At the same time, however, the Drones cheerfully imagined they would recover their entire purchase price when they sold their Rolling Knolls home. Oddly enough, the government itself had helped to foster the Drones' delusions.

"Much of today's housing demand comes not from new families, but from those seeking better and larger homes, and the typical two-bedroom postwar housing has now been replaced by the three-bedroom house in current production," Albert M. Cole, Housing and Home Finance Agency administrator, told the *Washington Star*.

"I believe we have crossed the threshold of a period of long delayed but urgently needed housing replacement and community improvement through which the needs of a large part of our existing population will, at last, be given effective attention.

"Mortgage financing is plentiful and the homebuilding rate is at a record high . . . I am confident . . . that the housing economy is basically strong."

It is certainly cheering to find so high a public officer anxious to meet the needs of an existing population, rather than those of a nonexistent populace, but when Mr. Cole speaks of houses as "in current production," something chills the soul. Surely here is a phrase that must have rolled off a General Motors assembly line. When houses are said to be in "production," one can only imagine "mass production." Mass-produced dwellings which, in turn, will produce mass dwellers. Developments, in short. Community improvement is certainly necessary in this fair land, and Mr. Cole is to be congratulated for wishing it to come about. But developments are not communities, as must be abundantly clear by this time, and there is no way on earth to improve them by means short of bulldozing.

Moreover, Mr. Cole seems to imply that families seeking greater living space can, and should, easily purchase the new homes now "in production" through the plentiful mortgage financing that is so much a part of the National Association of Home Builders' way of life. Just as though there was no alternative.

Meanwhile, Mr. Cole does not suggest what happens to those "typical two-bedroom postwar" houses when everyone plays musical chairs and jumps into the three-bedrooms in current production. For the answer to that one, we return you now to John Drone, at Rolling Knolls.

"Have you seen the people who bought the Wilds' house?" a startled John asked Mary Drone as he came home one night.

"Yes—they look awful; perfectly awful," Mary said.

"Yeah," John said. "Awful isn't the word for it. You should never go by first impressions, but I think in this case you can. I bet you if we ever thought Wild's back yard was a mess with all that junk in it, we'll wish he were back pretty soon."

"The place smells already," Mary said. She didn't know what the odor was, but it was certainly not that of fresh-baked bread, which used to drift into the morning air from Eve Wild's kitchen.

"And those horrid children," she went on. "Mrs. Voter told them to stop throwing stones at the bird box on her picket fence and the language they used at her was right out of the gutter. When Mrs. Voter went to see their mother about it, that new woman called her a nosey old bitch and told her to stay on her side of the street—that if anyone was going to tell her kids what to do, she'd do it."

"I heard there's another seedy-looking crew moved into that house that was up for sale on Kasserine Pass," John said. "I guess if we're going to get our money out of this place, we'd better get it while we can."

John Drone had never made better sense. It is a fundamental rule of real estate that there is no way for a neighborhood to go but down. Its best days are its infancy. Some neighborhoods last longer than others on their highest plateaus, but all, eventually, descend into the pit. In the case of the nation's jerry-built postwar developments, this process merely began sooner than in any other kind of community, including hobo jungles.

Since the nation had come to regard purchase of a new development house in the same light as purchase of a new car (it's good this year but we'll get rid of it next year), it became increasingly difficult from 1948 on to resell a development house to a man able (and the word is used loosely) to buy a brand-new development house. Newness became a criterion surpassing cost and, in some cases, need. Secondhand development houses were sold to the kind of people who buy secondhand automobiles solely out of need. People, in other words, less financially responsible; less able to give the same degree of care to the house than the original veteran-purchaser gave to it. This factor merely hastened Rolling Knolls' certain plunge to slumhood. Already many houses needed important repair. The Fecunds' house, for example, harbored termites.

Therefore the Drones redoubled their househunting efforts, examining every new suburban development with the wariness of those who, once bitten, are twice shy. Life in Fairfax County had taught them much.

"We want three bedrooms," John said. "OK. But let's make sure about a few other things, first.

"We have to be sure," he said, "that any place we buy isn't going to be rezoned tomorrow, or isn't next to a vacant lot that's been zoned for a factory last Tuesday, only nobody's told us about it. Next time, let's get a place with a sewer system we don't have to pay for. Let's find out whether there's any water, too. I never want to go through another summer like last year."

"That rationing was awful," Mary said. "Let's not think about Virginia any more. Mrs. Voter said the water table dropped ten to twenty feet in our area when that new development came in."

"And let's make sure the county or the state is going to keep up the roads," John said. "Remember those guys from Burmal's office who said the county would be glad to put the roads in, on an assessment basis? And then we found out the county didn't have a thing in the world to do with it,

THE FAINTS

THE AMIABLES

THE SPLEENS

THE FECUNDS

MRS. ARDIS
VOTER

. . . the personal inadequacy of her neighbors.

and that the state didn't have to do a thing, but that if we wanted the roads we would have to have them built at our own expense? I am getting damn tired of having to shell out each year to have the contractor come back and pour more hotpatch on the roads."

"We might ask whether there's any bus line near the place, and how far away the school is," Mary said. "We don't want to get caught again in a spot where they build the school after they build eight developments and the kids have to go double shifts over a clothing store till the school's ready."

"It would also be nice," John said, "to get a place that didn't flood every time it drizzles. Let's remember about storm sewers this time."

So the Drones thought about streets and utilities, and certain larger matters entirely escaped them. Mary found nothing strange in their search for a new house in another development. To her way of thinking, a larger house was therefore a better house; better houses cost more; better people had more money—*ergo*, a larger house necessarily stood in a better community. Mary attributed all her troubles to the inadequacy of her present house and the personal inadequacy of her neighbors. Dimly, she had felt the relationship between them, but she did not fully understand it. Her thinking—and therefore John's—was directed entirely toward newness, a third room, and money. Having learned full well all the lessons Fairfax County had to teach, she and John hunted exclusively among Maryland's burgeoning developments. And, in unthinking obedience to the dictates of current fad, they sought only the promised joys of split-level living.

"Everybody's buying split levels," was the way Mary put it.

Ah, well. There was a time when everybody bought those

ramblers that didn't ramble. In 1948, builders threw up slightly elongated boxes and called them ramblers. "Ramblers!" the signs said. "Turn right two blocks for Windswept Hills Ramblers!"

And now, in 1956 the signs said "Split Levels! Gargantuan Split Levels Just Ahead! Empire Colony Splits! Tri-Level Living At Its Finest! Turn Left, Follow Arrows to Wandras' Wondrous Split Levels!"

The genealogy of the split-level house in current production is out of a 1948 rambler by a root cellar. As John Drone had observed at Hardwood Forest, the builders had simply excavated a kind of half-basement and turned it into an extra room. They raised the ceiling of this room slightly above the living room level to become the floor of the bedroom level, and sometimes lowered the bedroom ceiling in compensation, in order not to have to split the roof. Thus the inhabitant of the split-level house could live partly underground, feed on the surface, and go up two steps to bed.

Mary and John Drone examined dozens of these ambiguous dens before finding the house, not of their dreams, but within an optimistic estimate of their means. They ignored the honest advice of Roland Suave whose employers, out of conscience or out of a simple desire to protect themselves, refused to sell their overpriced product to people who could not afford it. Fate led the Drones at last to that vast new development, Merryland Dell. It is a wonder they didn't turn to it sooner, for news of Merryland Dell was all about them. Eighteen times a day a Washington radio station broadcast the gladsome news in a singing commercial:

> "Come, come, come
> To the county . . .

Come to our Merryland Dell
For there in three or four le-eh-vels
Dwell dwellers of Merryland Dell."

As the music faded, a seductive contralto voice told you that if you had a house to sell or a house to trade, you could get hundreds and hundreds of dollars more than it was worth if you dealt with Razor the Trader on a Merryland Dell Split-Level Masterpiece. Or, even if you had no house to trade, you could still save hundreds and hundreds of dollars in purchasing a Merryland Dell dwelling. "Don't make a move," the rich voice sighed, "without seeing Razor the Trader for the sharpest deal in town."

Merryland Dell was that newest verge of a widening sea of houses spreading out through what had once been fat Montgomery County farmlands. The Drones arrived at the familiar muddy plain, the flag-bedecked sample house in the foreground, work crews in the middle distance, and bulldozers busy among the horizon's few remaining bits of greenery. Across the road from the sample house other bulldozers were busily creating the dirt fill on which was to rise the shopping center with its space for five thousand cars. A sporadic bus service, connecting with Washington buses, used the highway. A new school building was visible half a mile away from the sample house. Streets and sewers were in.

John, Mary, Kim and Chip joined the line of what real-estate promoters call "prospects." They saw the sampler. It had three bedrooms. It was new. It cost $17,500. John's heart curdled at the price, but the salesman told him not to worry about one little thing.

"Look," the salesman said very earnestly. "We know just

how it is. When Robert Razor started to build, he said to himself, 'I gotta build things folks can buy. I gotta give 'em more space. OK, so space costs money. But I gotta give 'em space and the price has got to be right.'

"That," the salesman said, "is right where Mr. Razor got his big idea. He'd make a trade."

And then, echoing the very words a spokesman for the Federal Housing Administration used to the author, the salesman told John Drone:

"A real-estate man who won't take a trade is dead. He's as dead as an automobile salesman who won't take a trade-in on a new car."

"I see," said John.

"Now lemme ask you this: How much equity you got in your present house?"

"About $3000," John said.

"Fine. Just fine," the salesman said, crossing his legs and regarding a suede shoe contemplatively. "That brings the price right down to $14,500. We'll sell your house for you, and take your equity as down payment. In other words, to you it's the same as nothing down. Now with taxes, insurance and settlement all thrown in, the monthly payments will run around $117 a month. How does that strike you? Hey? What's better than that?"

It struck John Drone like a bag of wet cement.

"It sounds all right," he said shakily. "But I guess we'll have to sleep on it and call you back."

"That's perfectly OK," the salesman said, rising and extending a hand. "Let me give you my card."

"Why, that monthly payment wasn't too far off what Hardwood Forest quoted us on a $22,000 house if we put out $3000 down," John told Mary that night.

"But Hardwood Forest wouldn't take us for nothing down unless we made $10,000 a year," Mary said, "and they wouldn't take us even with the down payment unless we made $7500."

"In many ways, this is a better deal," John said. "It doesn't have four bedrooms, but it does have three finished bedrooms."

"I don't know that I like having the third bedroom in the basement," Mary said, turning the matter over in her mind.

"It will be great," John said. "Chip can have the room to himself. He's getting to the age where a boy ought to be a little bit away from the family."

He busied himself with a pencil.

"Actually," he said, "we'll be coming out ahead. Next year we won't be carrying $660 worth of time payments. So it will cost us about $444 more to get the larger house. Really, we'll be saving that $200 in the middle. All the other expenses are just about the same as ours, now. Water, trash, sewage, utilities. The way I figure it, we'll get a larger house and actually save money."

Unfortunately for the Drones, that was not precisely the way things worked out; not according to Robert Razor's figuring.

"You mean you're not going to buy our house?" Mary asked the salesman the next day.

"Gosh, no, lady," he explained. "We're going to take it in trade. We'll sell it for you."

The Drones looked blankly at one another. Too late— they'd already signed an option.

"Now first," the salesman said, "we'll have to fix it up to sell it."

As things turned out, Mr. Razor's salesman decided all

the Drones' electrical appliances would have to be replaced. They couldn't take them with them—the new house came "completely equipped." The old appliances would also be traded in.

"People want new things," the salesman said. "Not these old models."

Six hundred dollars later, the new appliances were installed. They were purchased from Mr. Razor's pet jobber, but the Drones knew this not.

"Needs a new paint job," the salesman said. "Nobody's going to buy a falling-down-looking house."

Three hundred dollars later, the house was repainted; a reasonable price indeed. The painters were mercenaries from a distant realm of Mr. Razor's far-flung empire.

The house was sold, luckily enough, for $10,000. The salesman's commission of five per cent was exactly $500. It will be remembered the Drones had paid $10,500 for their house, but the salesman told them they could regard their $500 loss on resale as the rent they'd paid for the eight years they'd lived there. Cheap rent, he said with a smile.

In other words, the Drones paid out $1900 to sell their house to the pharmacist's assistant who bought it, assuming the Drones' GI mortgage. This left the Drones with $1100 to apply toward the purchase of their Merryland Dell $17,500 split level; not the $3000 on which their figures had depended. Thus, another ten dollars a month was added to their monthly mortgage payment calculations, and Drones' giddy visions of saving $200 a year on the move was diminished by $98.

It never occurred to John Drone that he would be firmly into his sixties before he finished paying for the new house, because neither John nor Mary thought for a moment of making their new address any more permanent than their old. Or, as Mary put it:

"It isn't what we want, exactly, but it will do for now. Someday the prices will come down."

Drone went back to the bank to hock his car to pay the mover. The bank was glad to do it—Drone's credit was just great.

Meanwhile, housing trades such as the Drones' are being made all across the nation. FHA spokesmen say the house trade-in "is the hottest thing in real estate. A number of [FHA] staff meetings have been held to discuss ways and means by which FHA facilities can be used to assist industry in carrying out the program."

While FHA sought means to help the builders with their little problems, it became increasingly apparent to John Drone that he could use a few more dollars—at least another thousand a year. But where, and how, to get it? Drone's rise in government service had been meteoric. Already he had his own glass-partitioned cubicle in Census Bureau. In twenty or thirty years, he might aspire to an office with a door, a bookcase, and a color photograph of the then current President. Perhaps even a secretary. But for vast reaches of years ahead, it was only too obvious he would earn $5500 a year. Naturally, it was Mary who read the want ads.

"It says here, government employee wanted as retail liquor store salesman, nights and Saturdays," she read. "Apply Box Y182."

Virtue, and John's unprepossessing appearance, were rewarded. For three nights a week, half a day Saturdays, John labored in The Vineyard, Washington's Cut-Rate Bottlery. He by no means spent all of that extra twenty dollars a week on the extra commuting.

Owning property implies a certain permanence.

And, acting again on Mary's sharp-tongued advice, John worked as a temporary, part-time salesman for Sears, Roebuck during the Christmas rush, and so earned the family's Yuletide money. It was as though the Drones had forsaken their tissue-paper boat and John was now carrying them all on his back as he struck out briskly for shore. The shore, however, kept edging away as he swam, for shortly after they'd moved into Merryland Dell, the county tax base was sharply reassessed—upwards, naturally. And the children were growing like weeds, in constant need of new clothing. And the pressures of their new community were great. For one thing, Mary had discovered that in Merryland Dell, people served wine and brandy with their meals when they entertained one another. And at a dinner party in Merryland Dell, roast beef took the place of Rolling Knolls casserole. When John's decrepit car gave up the ghost, Mary persuaded him it was folly to buy another cheap car, and pointed out that in Merryland Dell the taste ran more to new Buicks than to secondhand Fords. Wherefore, John splashed on and on across the vasty deep, and ever did that farther shore recede.

We have seen that the pattern of Mary Drone's days at Rolling Knolls added up to boredom and despair, but what now shall we say of the pattern of John's days at Merryland Dell?

He rose at six and raced downtown to try to find an all-day parking space near his office. He knew perfectly well that if he didn't arrive on the scene at seven, there would be no space available. Here it must be said the Washington situation is unusual—the city is not served by commuter trains, and each day all the cars from all the developments for miles and miles around come grinding into town.

Having parked, John went for a little walk along Washington's early streets, delaying for as long as possible the time he would have to go to the Coffee Spout for breakfast. It is very hard to make breakfast last two hours, even while smoking and having extra cups of coffee and reading the *Washington Post* and talking with colleagues. So first John walked, and then surrendered to the Coffee Spout.

He arrived at his office at nine and worked steadily on yesterday's correspondence for two whole hours. It was then time for the midmorning coffee break, and time to read the *Washington Daily News*. He resumed his pencil-buying chores at noon, worked another hour until lunchtime, returned from this at two, and entertained notions of sleep until the midafternoon coffee break. At four thirty he raced to his parked car and became involved in Washington's inchworm rush-hour traffic. He was home at six, bolted supper, and thrice a week dashed downtown again for his tour of duty in The Vineyard. He was home just after midnight for a good night's rest. On those days when he did not labor in The Vineyard he went to bed promptly after supper. Half his Saturday was spent in gainful labor, and Sunday was his own—unless Mary wanted him to take the family out for a drive, which she usually did.

John Drone thus ordered his days; bent Life to his will, so to speak—grasped this sorry scheme of things entire and molded it closer to his heart's desire. His earthly reward was something like $6500 a year before taxes, and because of his extra duties at Sears, Christmas came free. Drone was a good provider, in the sense that he was awfully good at trying to provide the better things in life for his family.

Because of John's efforts, the family had a three-bedroom house, an unpaid-for new Buick, a television set, a kitchen full of electrical wonders, food in its deepest freeze. It did not have more delightful vacations, or more frequent nocturnal amusement, or any greater number of new clothes, and except for infrequent occasions, the diet was distressingly familiar. The family had less of a father and husband than at any prior time, but in all candor, it must be reported John Drone found this just as well. He was given to counting his blessings, and if you'd asked him how he was making out, he would have said:

"Great. I have a wife and two swell kids, a new split level with everything in it, a new car with all the extras, and I got myself not one but three jobs. I'm meeting all my payments, every month."

As for Mary's life, the first few weeks were spent in the charming exhilaration which new surroundings always bring. Gaily, she explored the cellar bedroom which had been added to her domain. She liked the little thrill of going up two steps to the living room, and then up another two into the bedrooms. She was as happy as a squirrel in a new, three-ring cage. This light mood persisted through nearly two months, until at last there came that day when her new world suddenly became only too familiar.

It was the day she stood looking out her picture window and for the first time became completely aware of the picture window across the treeless street. For a horrid moment she stood there, staring. Then she ran to her door and tore it open, looking up and down the block. And everywhere she looked, she saw houses exactly like her own, row on row of them, the same, the same, the same . . .

6. Here We Go Again

"A house is not a home."—Polly Adler

MARY DRONE was trying to bring order out of Chip's basement room when there was a brisk staccato on her new front door. On the steps Mary encountered a stringy woman in tweeds and a pearl necklace; a woman who transfixed Mary with a glittering eye and whose small talk was a gust of rifle fire.

"I'm sorry we're so long in getting acquainted," she told Mary. "I'm Mrs. Hamilton Surge and I'd like to know what you're going to do about the school situation the school they built is six classrooms too small now the county says it isn't going to spend any more money in our area we want you as a mother and as a taxpayer and as a voter to join us in the Beleaguered Women can you meet with us in my house four-six-one-seven Gardenia Avenue at ten tomorrow morning?"

And then, before Mary could reply, Mrs. Surge added: "Not only that, but they don't teach the children to read or write."

"I'm afraid not," Mary broke in, feeling desperately as

though she'd lived this moment, too, somewhere, sometime in the past.

"They certainly don't," Mrs. Surge agreed. "They use some kind of silly flash cards instead of teaching the child how words are made out of letters and how the sounds——"

"I mean I'm afraid I can't come," Mary blurted. "I'll be busy in the morning; I'll have one child home.

"It's those split sessions," Mary explained, seeing contempt burst into finest flower in Mrs. Surge's long face. "For years I looked forward to the day when both children would be in school, and in our last development there were split sessions so I had them both home practically as soon as I got the house picked up in the morning.

"We moved here because the school was so new and so big and close," she went on, "and then we found there were still split sessions. Now Chip goes to school in the morning and Kim goes in the afternoon, and I'm stuck here all the time."

"Well, there you are," Mrs. Surge said complacently. "Your problem is our problem—ours is yours—and it's never going to get better unless we get together to do something about it we're not going to let them get away with it so come to my house tomorrow and bring your child along the children can all play in the lower-level room together."

Mrs. Surge rattled on and on. It seems the county school board had wisely anticipated yet-unbuilt Merryland Dell's population when they let the contract for the new school building. But between the time the contract was granted and the building was completed, three new developments— Happy Heights, Pleasant Dale and Sunny Mede—had burst out of the earth just north of the school grounds. Thus, when the new school opened, it was hopelessly overcrowded. It all sounded dreadfully familiar to Mary.

"I'd like to know what you're going to do about the school situation."

"Well, I'll see," Mary said wearily. "I hope I can make it."
Mrs. Surge eyed her suspiciously, and left.

The following morning Mary's phone rang at ten o'clock, but she did not answer it for fear it would be Mrs. Surge. (It was.) Although Mary knew full well she should take an interest in public matters—particularly in those which affected her so intimately—she couldn't bring herself to attend the meeting. Let's let other people think about these things for a change, she told herself. The newness of her house had worn off and Mary was again deep in the clutches of Development Ennui, the Black Plague of our time. She'd already decided she wasn't going to live in Merryland Dell a minute longer than she had to; she refused (again) to imagine that ownership of a house implied any permanence of mailing address, and, buoyed by this sense of irresponsibility, divorced herself from the new development's common causes.

In this curious mental process, Mary was unconsciously following the attitude of John Drone and most development men. The men had no allegiance. They couldn't be less interested in Washington's community problems, because the city was just a place they visited each day to earn enough to cover their time payments. They couldn't be less interested in their developments, because to them, the development was just a place to eat and sleep near their work—as impersonal, if not as convenient, as an hotel.

The source of Mary's ennui was not confined to a boredom with community problems, however. Her trouble was that in every way, Merryland Dell was as stifling a place as Rolling Knolls. Except for that extra bedroom and the brick construction, you couldn't tell the difference between the developments without a road map. Once again there was no recreational area, no cohesive center of neighborly interest. There were identical houses on identical streets. Fences appeared around the yards. Husbands underwent matutinal extirpation in absentia at the lawn date. Things were different only in degree, and everyone went marching over the threshold of boredom in lockstep.

In Merryland Dell, Mary discovered, boredom cost more than in Rolling Knolls. She found out that social life was slightly beyond her means, but it was also beyond the means of everyone else. Still, everyone in Merryland Dell thought everyone else surely must be able to afford it because everyone had a $17,500 house, so no one dared throw the kind of bring-your-own-bottle party so popular in Rolling Knolls. Instead, they relentlessly poisoned one another with Martinis—the cheapest and most virulent man-bane known to toxicology.

The cocktail parties split as easily into two groups as they had at Rolling Knolls, and if the jokes were a bit more coarse, the innuendoes a little more obvious, the cocktail party was still the same recognizable institution.

The drapes across the picture windows, the prints on the walls—these were a bit more expensive, but equally as uniform. The shopping center was—well, it was another shopping center. Mary's soul did not dance with joy as she trundled her tiny tumbrel among the impersonal aisles of standard brands, helping herself twice a week to the advertised good things of this life in the supermarket.

In short, Mary's ennui stemmed from the same sources which fed the ennui of Rolling Knolls. In Merryland Dell there was once again physical monotony, the enforced intimacy with neighbors, the homogeneity of the inhabitants, the constantly expressed desire to move "sooner or later," and—most of all—complete surrender of social and neighborhood affairs to a disillusioned, inexperienced, inept, frustrated matriarchy.

This last point cannot be overemphasized. The fact that developments have created matriarchal societies has interested, if not worried the daylights out of, a good many trained observers, and for a good many different reasons. One of the worried men is Dr. Leonard J. Duhl, National Institute of Mental Health psychiatrist, who wonders what kind of future generations will emerge from the houses in current production. He wondered out loud, and at length, to the American Society of Planning Officials, meeting in Montreal on September 28, 1955.

"Suburbia," said Dr. Duhl, using a genteel word for housing developments, "typifies the changes taking place in American society. . . The course it is taking may leave its imprint not only on the physical scene, but also on the minds and health of men."

Then, plunging to the heart of the matter, he said: "Suburbia is a bedroom area, in most instances, with people working in the city. Father races out of the house early in the morning on his way to work, not to return till late at night, and leaves mother not only to care for the home, but to be the ruler of daytime suburbia. This, then, is a matriarchal society, with children who know men only as nighttime residents and weekend guests.

"Why should such a feminine, maternal environment be possibly detrimental to the growth of children? A child, in order to grow, needs a multiplicity of experiences and participation in activities with both sexes in order to learn from seeing how others act or behave. Boys, for example, need to identify with their fathers by figuratively placing themselves in father's shoes. Similarly, girls need to have fathers in order to learn how they, as women-to-be, should react to men.

"Suburbia's absence of fathers differs from similar situations in the city in that the cities offer more people, other than fathers, to identify with. Suburbias don't have this. . .

"Not only is the child left to this entirely feminine world," Dr. Duhl said, "but he also is in a world free of different people. Minority groups being out of place—they may be classified as an oddity. Grandparents and older people are often absent, too. Those around him are children of the same age, with mothers who all left school around the same time.

"To compound the problem, Junior is faced with a culture made up of children whose families are usually in the same economic bracket, and with fathers who may even have similar occupations. Ofttimes this is true not only in the immediate area of his home but also in relation to his schoolmates as well. Not only does he have little close contact with different types of people, but he doesn't often rub shoulders with them or even see them.

"Thus we have a segregated, one-socio-economic-level, matriarchal society that offers limited experience to the growing child. For optimal development, children need multiple experiences. Not only is each child different at birth, but he will never find his ultimate capacities and capabilities unless exposed to many experiences; get a chance to try out new ideas, feelings and himself, to see what fits. . .

"At the same time as saying that the developing child needs many experiences—I wonder whether the eternal movements in suburbia, with people constantly changing residences and cities, is conducive to his optimal health. Similarly, the social pressure for upward social movement from house to bigger house may undermine to some extent the security of the child."

Then, shifting his attack, Dr. Duhl discussed that most obvious of all development influences, creeping mental paralysis.

"In our society," he said, "and this is certainly not true of suburbia alone, there is ever-increasing pressure for conformity. Despite the ever-increasing choice of things to buy and own, man is pressured to conform. Advertisements fall in with his own need to keep up with the Joneses; his job is increasingly more routinized and perhaps boring; his recreation, in part, is given to him in packets such as TV and the movies.

"Schools, because of the tremendous desire for more education, have put their emphasis on 'over-all programs' for all, with little chance to encourage individuality and spontaneity. Perhaps, then, suburbia adds to the present cultural pressure to conformity and doesn't allow enough of the individual to show himself. We may soon be forced to recognize the need for this, as we need more and more gifted people to develop new ideas and methods for our society. There is a wastage of talent—as we cry for more scientists, doctors, engineers, etc. Our communities contribute to the problem. . .

"A growing child," Dr. Duhl warned, "needs encouragement for his ideas and even for some of his daydreams. If his schools, because of tremendous work loads, can't offer him this through new educational experiences, he may suffer. He needs encouragement and stimulation. Schools with sufficient teachers and facilities that are free to spend time with him can do this. The community, by offering a multiplicity of experiences which will really be used through clubs, centers, libraries, etc., can similarly help."

When he speaks of a community, Dr. Duhl begins to edge into the sociologist's domain. Certainly anyone is free to draw his own sociological conclusions, and Dr. Duhl may be better qualified than most to do so, but just for form's sake, let's chuck the ball back to a live, certified sociologist—our trusty familiar, Harold Mendelsohn. Mr. Mendelsohn is also interested in the ways developments are changing the patterns of American life, and like Dr. Duhl, he's worried about the developments' influence on our young.

"In a normal community," Mr. Mendelsohn said nostalgically, "there would be YMCA and church facilities for dances, sports and social life; there would be public libraries —even corner stores. In the modern development the houses are too small for young families. Today's families can't entertain at home now, and when today's children are teen-age, where do you suppose they will hold *their* parties and normal social life? They certainly won't be able to conduct it anywhere in a development that is simply a lot of houses.

"To a sociologist," Mr. Mendelsohn said, "a community is a cohesive entity that supplies essential needs and services to all the people who live in it. In developments, we have already seen that churches are nonexistent or too few; that parks and recreational area are most often missing. These developments are just bedrooms on the edge of town. What do you suppose will happen when the preschool children in all these places are ten years older? Where will they go, and what will they do? You know perfectly well they will find all their pleasures outside the development.

"Since even the movies are often miles away in the shopping center at the other end of the development, you know the only thing for tomorrow's children will be to borrow the family car. In other words, *all* their recreation will be away from home. There will be no chance for them to associate home with fun. To them, fun will always mean something that happens away from home—away from any sort of parental supervision.

"Not all the features of a development are bad," Mr. Mendelsohn said judiciously. "For one thing, there is no question that the development is a far healthier place to live than the tenement or row house on a dingy, traffic-choked industrial street. Crime rates in the development areas are insignificant at present. Of course, what the crime rate will be ten years from now when the children grow up with no place to meet or play under adult supervision is something else again."

Another moody observer of the national scene is Dr. John R. Cavanagh, a psychiatrist, who told the twenty-fourth National Catholic Family Life Conference, meeting in Boston on March 13, 1956, that development life may well breed divorce. He, too, was disturbed by the possible fate of the development child. Development life, he said, contains factors "which few husbands and wives realize frustrate their parental role.

"They think that moving from crowded city conditions to semi-rural areas is a real contribution to their children's welfare," he said.

"It can, on the contrary, make the children psychological orphans. Longer traveling time to and from the job and school allows little time for the family at home. Late working conditions may prevent the father from seeing his children for days on end."

Dr. Cavanagh, like Dr. Duhl and every other development observer, noticed man's abandonment of the development to the ladies, and found it ominous.

"The father," he said, "has an obligation to contribute more than money to the upbringing of the children. His wife needs him to be dependent upon—when man abdicated his responsibility in the home, he forced his wife into a position of leadership for which she is not prepared. At the same time, the male children were deprived of parental supervision. This too frequently results in weak, passive males inadequate to take over the leadership in the home because they never learn independence of female leadership."

Miss Elizabeth O'Malley, director of Montgomery County (Maryland) Social Service League, isn't so sure that most development men didn't arrive on the scene weak, passive and inadequate. Her office is surrounded by a wilderness of housing developments, and she deals every day with the problems of their inhabitants. Naturally, she's drawn certain conclusions from her experience.

"The concept of suburbia in general is a woman-dominated field," she said. "Women are almost entirely influential. The suburbs are, however, also largely populated by dependent, childish husbands. The usual pattern is that the wife is an aggressive person trying to create a home of her own. She gets him to buy a house they're really not able to buy, economically. She pushes him to the point where he weakens, buys the place, and then finds himself in debt. Thereupon, she nags him for having bought a house they couldn't afford."

In abandoning the development to the woman, the man usually abandons political considerations as well, Miss O'Malley said, allowing the woman to make up his mind for him on candidates and issues.

"On election day it is usual for a development woman to meet her husband on his way home from work and tell him to go right off to the polling booth. The chances are he has taken no interest in local politics and has no idea of the issues. His wife will hand him a list of candidates she prefers—that is, candidates acceptable to her women's group. He'll take the list and go to the booth and his wife, in other words, will have cast two votes."

Not all suburban women are masterful creatures, but all nonetheless inherit exactly as much responsibility as the husband abandons. Many development women are neurotic, Miss O'Malley said, and their neuroses are deepened by the homogeneity of the neighborhood. In brooding on the inadequacy of their lives, many become physically ill, and Miss O'Malley suspects quite a few of these mind-made sicknesses are attention-getting devices.

"I have had women come to my office saying 'Oh, if I could just get away for a couple of hours to be myself again —I've given up all my city friends—it's my husband's fault for moving us out here.' The development is simply no place for a whining woman," Miss O'Malley said. "It is no place for a woman without resources of her own."

While Mr. Mendelsohn and Drs. Duhl and Cavanagh remarked on the national scene, Miss O'Malley spoke only on the basis of her observations of life in Montgomery County developments. But Montgomery County contains several different price levels of developments, and Miss O'Malley— whose office provides family counseling to anyone who needs it, rich or poor—is therefore in an excellent position to throw a little further light on a fairly gloomy canvas. While our other observers spoke of "developments" or "suburbia" in general, Miss O'Malley is able to pick out social-problem patterns within the various development strata. To be sure, an expensive development contains the same major sources of human discord as a cheap development, but "different developments seem to produce different problems," Miss O'Malley said.

"In the cheaper, lower-class developments, where most of the homeowners are young or fairly futile, almost all the problems are economic. These people are deep in the toils of the loan sharks, and the lack of conscience of business firms in pressuring these people already in debt to buy more things on time is simply unbelievable.

"In the middle-priced developments, you begin to get into the parent-child relationship problems; the extramarital affairs. On the middle level, where most people have been married for, say, seven years, there's apt to be the affair with the woman in the car pool—that's quite common around this Rockville area. It usually comes about after the cocktail party with its dirty jokes. The woman nags her husband for having made a fool of himself, and in so doing, drives him right into the arms of someone else.

"In the upper level, people are apt to be more sophisticated in finding answers to their problems," Miss O'Malley said. "The father has his business, the mother her social or community affairs, and the children are taught to have some activity purely their own. Thus, the family (with the best intentions in the world) is widely separated. If the children seem unhappy, the family answers this problem by packing them off to a boarding school. If the parents have problems, they take them to their psychiatrists."

Miss O'Malley observed that people in different economic classes have different problems at different times of their lives. In the homogenous development, however, it would seem that everyone comes down with the same problems at the same time, like so many coolies suffering recurring bouts of cholera. Such is the case, she said, with any development, whether it is a rickety collection of $5000 boxes or an isolated bevy of $50,000 split levels. Once again, in yet another way, the homogenous nature of a development reinforces a problem, for if bitter truth be known, misery really doesn't like company. Company just makes misery more miserable than ever.

Meanwhile, Miss O'Malley is as much disturbed over the development child's uncertain future as any other professional person. Children, she said, reflect their homes—happy children come from a happy home. Many development children are distinctly unhappy and insecure, she finds, reflecting their parents' tensions and economic worries.

"The children come home from school and find their parents out. Mother and father in both lower- and middle-income levels are apt to be out working to pay off their debts.

"The children are left to their own resources. There are no grandparents in developments—the house is hardly big enough for the family as it is. Perhaps a neighbor will look after the children—keep an eye out for them—perhaps not. There is no recreational area. There is no place for the children to play but in the yard, which is too small, or in the street. The children come home to an empty house and can't help feeling pushed aside and insecure. It is out of such conditions that delinquency develops."

The enormous question of the development child's fate when he bursts into adolescence is still a few years off in most places throughout the nation, but Miss O'Malley is already getting the first dose of it, since one of the nation's first, worst, and cheapest developments, built just after the war, is fast becoming a slum in her Montgomery County. The thing to remember in this regard is that the difference in developments—and their inhabitants—is only one of minor degree, as Miss O'Malley points out.

In the face of these competent opinions, it would appear

that a housing development is just no fit place for man, woman or child. It would seem that Mary and John Drone, in moving to a new development, were once again batting on the stickiest of wickets; that they were literally placing their family health—mental, moral and physical—in the clammy hands of Razor the Trader when they re-embarked on development life. Such would seem the opinion of the professionals.

On the other hand, it is quite possible that such worrywarts as sociologists, social workers and psychiatrists are completely mistaken in their estimate. Surely all those advertisements promising "gracious living" can't be wrong. Surely there must be a brighter side to this picture; surely an author's implacable search will discover one.

Well, as a matter of fact, there *are* disinterested observers who look upon developments and find nothing but good things to say about them. The Honorable Joel T. Broyhill, U.S. Representative for the northern Virginia district, is such a man. A forthright fellow, Representative Broyhill was glad to publish his encouraging opinions in a signed article in the *Washington Post* last April 22.

> In commenting briefly on our progress and prospects for the future [*he wrote*], I would be remiss if I did not point with pride and give credit to the building and construction industry. These public-spirited developers have adhered religiously to a policy of providing "the best that money can buy."
>
> The best interests of the home buyer motivate their every action, and without such a commendable attitude, our progress would be obstructed.
>
> As the Congressman from northern Virginia, I extend my sincere good wishes to my thousands of neighbors who are finding joy and contentment in our numerous communities. To those additional thousands who will join us soon in our splendid neighborhoods, I extend a hearty welcome.

They will discover, as we before them have already discovered, the glory and wonders of suburban living. They will find peace and happiness and join our swelling chorus of "Hi, Neighbor!"

Now, surely no one would suggest that Representative Broyhill's views would in any way be colored by the fact he is related to M. T. Broyhill, the builder, whose houses were singled out for such exhaustive attention by the Teague committee's report. Representative Broyhill is a legislator beyond such reproach, and it is doubly valuable to have his views of housing developments because, among other things, they represent another Congressional point of view.

Neither John nor Mary Drone read this article, which is unfortunate, for it might have sustained them in certain dark days that yet lay in the womb of Time. As a matter of fact, they didn't read any paper very thoroughly. Mary confined herself to the women's section to seek out the newest, least suspected household thrill, and John read the sport pages with the misplaced optimism of the Washington baseball fan. He also sought some new, unsuspected thrill, and his chances of finding it were just as good in the sport section as Mary's chances among the menus.

Meanwhile, the pattern of their days was the pattern of development days, as we have seen. At some future time, Mary hoped, they could take one of those fly-now-pay-later trips to Europe that everybody seemed to be taking. But she didn't know what she would do with the children. Everyone said Europe was so dirty and you had to be careful what you ate.

Still, she dreamed of soaring over the glinting Atlantic to those history-shrouded shores. Next year, maybe, they could do it—when the car was paid for. It is just as well she didn't know what Fate, the old jokesmith, had in store.

7. Goodbye, Mr. Drone

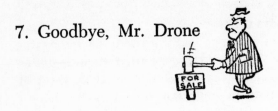

"And so we say farewell to these happy natives."—Robert Benchley

DR. JOSEPH LEECH, M.D., was a dark-haired, thin, young man whose movements were as brisk and precise as his speech.

"There's not a thing in the world wrong with you, young lady," he told Mary Drone. He grinned a knowing little grin. "You know what it is, don't you? Congratulations!"

"You mean . . . I'm pregnant?" Mary breathed.

"Just as pregnant as they ever come," Dr. Leech said gaily. "I'll see you in the delivery room, oh, let's say around March fifteenth, give or take a day. Any particular hospital you'd like in town?"

"My God," Mary said.

She wandered numbly back from Dr. Leech's shopping-center office to her Merryland Dell split-level masterpiece.

Pregnant!

It was ridiculous. Why, she had one child nearly twelve years old; the second was nearly eight.

They hadn't planned on it at all. It must have been—it

must have been that night just after they'd moved in when they were laughing about the new house, and John had jumped up and down the two stairs like a little boy and afterwards they'd taken a chance and she knew she was taking a chance but John said the odds were way in their favor.

Well, they'd taken a chance, all right. It was perfectly ridiculous that this should happen now.

Mary spent the rest of her day on the edge of tears, and everything she did, everything she saw, reminded her of the overwhelming fact. She ironed John's shirts and thought of diapers. They didn't have any diapers. Years and years ago she thought she'd seen the last of diapers. Diapers and baby bottles and bottle brushes and bathinettes and a baby basket and blankets and then a crib, a crib mattress and pad, rubber sheets, rubber pants, baby clothes, a stroller, baby toys, baby lotions, clogged nipples at two A.M., trips to the pediatrician, formulas—all to do all over again. She wasn't young any more, she told herself desperately. You have to be young to stand it.

Mary folded up the ironing and went to the writing desk to make out a shopping list. She guessed it was her pregnancy that had made her forget to do the shopping when she went to see Dr. Leech at the shopping center. She took up a pen and it reminded her of bills. There would be Dr. Leech's bill, and the hospital bill, and what that hospital bill would be she dared not think. Their medical insurance policy paid only a third of the costs incurred in delivery. Then there would be the medicine to buy and the pediatrician to pay.

She stared absently out her picture window and saw lawns full of young mothers and babies. That, she realized, was just where she'd be—again. Out on the lawns with the mothers, talking about toilet-training. She could look forward to at least four more years of it, and just when she'd thought she'd reached a point in life where there would be a little time to herself with both children in school.

Listlessly, she tried to concentrate on her shopping list again. Chip would very shortly be home from school—she'd leave a note saying where she was. Chip—that third bedroom!

For the first time in her married life, Mary had a house that provided just enough space for all members of her family, and now there would not be space enough. Where would they put the baby? They could keep it in their room —they'd *have* to keep it in their room—at least through the night-feeding stage. Then, depending on whether it was a boy or girl, they could put it in with either Chip or Kim. Either way, one child wouldn't have a room to himself any more, just when both children were at the age when they really needed rooms to themselves for their homework, and for their growing sense of privacy. But what else could they do? Their split-level masterpiece didn't come with an expansible attic. Maybe they should look—not that they could buy it yet—for a four-bedroom house somewhere.

Mary made up her list, wrote a note for Chip; told Kim, who was leaving for the afternoon session, to watch out crossing the streets, and wandered toward the shopping center again.

In a daze she plodded down Iris Street to Gardenia, then to Rosebud, and so out Daffodil to the corner to wait for traffic to clear on the superhighway. I'd better enjoy the walk while I can, she told herself. She thought of the days ahead when she would have to push a stroller over the route. Mary hated taking babies to the supermarket.

It wasn't having the baby she minded, Mary told herself. She liked babies. But they did tie a woman down so. Next time she had a baby, she thought, she wanted to be in a place that she didn't mind so much, because you're stuck in your house or in your neighborhood when you have a baby. What kind of sense does that make? she asked herself. Well, she answered her mind, you know what I mean. . .

That day, the supermarket was featuring a sale on canned baby foods. Mary very nearly bought some, because of the sale, then decided against it because there was no room for such luxuries on her weekly shopping budget. How, she wondered, would they ever pay for it? Oh yes—the car might be paid for by then. There would be no fly-now-pay-later trip to Europe next year. Not for another seven years, at the very least.

I must think of other things, Mary told herself. What, she thought, would she tell John when he came home that night?

Meanwhile, as Mary sorted through her jumbled mind, John Drone's phone rang at Census Bureau. The sudden sound jarred him wide awake.

"Pencil procurement, Drone speaking," he said, pulling himself together.

"Are you the same John Drone who sold a house at Thirteen Bataan, Rolling Knolls Estates, to an S. M. Shifty of Bedsprings, Arkansas, a pharmacist's assistant?" a bored voice asked.

"Ye-e-ss."

"Well, this is Howard Catchpoll of SOB Suburban Bank and Trust," the voice said. "I got some bad news for you, Drone. It looks like that house is your baby again."

"What do you mean, my baby again?"

"Shifty never met the last three monthly payments," Mr.

Catchpoll said. "We went there to ask him how come, and there's no doubt about it—he's skipped out.

"We got a key and went in," Mr. Catchpoll said, "and bro-ther, did he ever make a mess of that place. God knows where they ate, because they sure didn't use the stove. There isn't any stove. That bird must have sold the appliances on his way out. We checked up where he's been working, and it seems he just left town without telling his boss where he'd left the dough that had been in the cash register."

"Aren't the police doing anything?" Drone asked.

"Oh, sure. They're poking around somewhere in Arkansas, looking for him. But there's nothing we're going to be able to do but yank the joint back and toss it back to you."

"To me? How come? Shifty bought the place, didn't he? I'm out of it. I sold it. That's up to you and Shifty," Drone pleaded.

"Look, Drone," Mr. Catchpoll said. "You don't get it. Shifty just assumed your GI mortgage. That mortgage was insured in your name. In other words, the government said to us, 'We got faith in Drone, so we're insuring part of his mortgage to you.' OK—so you let Shifty take over your mortgage. But it's still your mortgage. So now the payments are behind. OK. We heave Shifty out, and now you got the place back."

"Hey!" Drone gasped. "Wait a minute. You mean *you* got the place. You hold the mortgage, don't you?"

"We sure do," Mr. Catchpoll agreed. "What I'm saying all along is we hold *your* mortgage. You still have $7500 to pay on it, at four per cent.

"Now there are a couple of things we can do, Drone," the cold voice said. "We can sell it for what we can, and you can make up the difference at the old rate of sixty-five dollars a month. I really couldn't say what we'd get for it, the shape it's in. Or," Mr. Catchpoll suggested, "we can just deed it back to you, and you just go on with your payments like nothing's happened. Then, if you don't want to live in the place, you can fix it up and rent it."

"You mean it's really mine?" Drone asked.

"It sure as hell is," Mr. Catchpoll said.

"Why don't I sell it to you?" Drone asked. "You know it's worth $10,500 because that's what you sold it to me for. Then you could sell it again, or rent it."

"Oh, for God's sake, Drone," Mr. Catchpoll said irritably. "We're not in the junk business. We don't want the lousy house. We built the houses to sell for $10,500—what we want is the profit on that sale and a return of interest on our investment. We couldn't sell one of those Rolling Knolls houses for $10,000 today, and we wouldn't even try. Let me give you my name and number and you can call me back and tell me what you want to do about it. Then we'll make an appointment."

"Yes, I'll want to talk it over with my wife," Drone said.

"Sure you do, sure you do," Mr. Catchpoll agreed. "We understand. It's tough, but that's how it is."

John spent the rest of his day in a vacuum. He drove home automatically, inching along in the traffic, completely oblivious of the stifling heat. When he shambled up his front steps, he still hadn't thought of what he was going to say to Mary.

She met him at the door and they kissed, as usual. He looked at Mary's stricken face and realized something was wrong.

"You've heard?" he began.

"Yes," Mary said. "The doctor . . . the doctor said we're going to have a baby."

The rest of the day was spent in a vacuum.

She looked at him with brimming eyes and seemed about to wilt. John folded her in his arms.

"Oh," he said. "Oh. That's fine . . . fine . . . isn't it?"

"Well," she said, "I guess there goes that trip to Europe next year."

"We got anything to drink?" John asked.

"I'll go look," Mary said.

John stood in his living room, idly rummaging through his pockets. The suit was newly back from the cleaners, and John felt an unremembered bit of pasteboard in his right pocket. He took it out and looked at it carefully. It was a little blurry and rumpled, but there was no question what it was.

It was his lifetime membership card in the Rolling Knolls Pool.

8. Here's Cheer, Mates

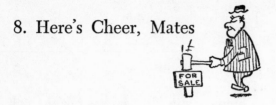

"Citoyens, aux armes!"—Paris street cry

MERCY, and other practical considerations, should prevent us from following John and Mary Drone down, down into the Slough of Despond, the dismal fen that is the natural haunt of the skip-tracer, the repossessor, the flint-eyed usurer. These are good times, happy times! No one wants to hear, today, of a family selling its television set, selling its new car, living on three-day-old bread and barley water, the children dressed in rags, gnawing cold potato skins in the school cafeteria while their more fortunate schoolmates buy the hot lunch. No—books should end happily, so let us leave the Drones perched on their highest peak, the owners (so to speak) of a new Buick, sparkling electrical appliances and two houses; living the American dream and happily awaiting the birth of a new heir.

Besides, Drone has served us well. In T. S. Eliot's words, he has been an easy tool, deferential, glad to be of use, politic, cautious and meticulous—but a bit obtuse; at times, indeed, almost ridiculous—almost, at times, the fool. But basically a good guy. We wish him well.

Anyway, we have other fish to fry. You have patiently followed a murky tome that has posed several questions in its
own rancid way, and in all common decency you are entitled
to such answers as there are. There are no easy answers,
which is just as well, for if there seemed to be a simple
resolution to the problems of development life, it would un-
doubtedly become a new fad and we'd be off and away,
sprinting like crazy toward a new form of mediocrity.

Generally speaking, our problems fall into two major cate-
gories: those posed by developments already in existence;
those posed by developments to come. And coming they are,
for we're assured by government and industrial estimates
that the end of the building boom is not in sight. As *U.S.*

. . . sprinting like crazy toward a new form of mediocrity.

News & World Report headlined it last March 2, "RUSH
TO SUBURBS JUST STARTING . . . SENSATIONAL
GROWTH AHEAD IN NEXT 20 YEARS." We can certainly
act now to control the shape and size of future developments,
but before we get to that matter, let's consider what—if
anything—can be done to make the boxes in current production better places in which to live. It will be remembered
that Mary Drone's difficulties in Rolling Knolls stemmed
from the fact that her house, her neighbors and her neighborhood were each inadequate. First of all, let's consider her
too-small house.

The Japanese have lived for centuries in houses that lack
what Americans would call adequate living space, and that
lack any standards of privacy we know. Furthermore, Japanese houses sit even closer together than our most crowded
developments. Over the millennia, the Japanese have worked
out some curious solutions to the problems they share with
Mary Drone.

By doing away with practically all furniture, including
beds, Japanese homes seem relatively spacious. The rooms
are peculiarly adaptable (to borrow a phrase from the real-
estate boys) because they can be used for any purpose
whatsoever. Suppertime? Just bring the charcoal brazier into
the living room, sit on the floor around it, cook and eat.
Remove the cooking pots and the room is a living room again.
Later, pull out a couple of wooden pillows, unroll the sleeping mats, and *voilà!* it's the master bedroom. No closets
necessary, please; storage bins located under honorable trap
door in floor.

The Japanese are no bears about drawing the blinds,
despite the fact that their neighbors three feet away could
peek in any time they so desired. It would simply never

occur to the neighbors to do so. Lacking space for privacy, the Japanese have cultivated the illusion of privacy to such a point that their privacy is as real as though they were each locked into separate, soundproofed American bathrooms. Japanese just pretend they're all alone in this world and turn their attention inward, on their family, where the bulk of the family's attention certainly belongs.

In every Japanese house there is the *tokonoma,* the honored alcove. This displays the family's work of art. No family is too poor to boast such an alcove, for that work of art is nearly always handmade. It may be a flower arrangement, an illuminated scroll, a poem, a painting. But whatever the work, it represents in every way the spirit of the family.

Without condemning Mary Drone to sleep on the deck with her neck on a log, we can borrow a few ideas from the Oriental development dwellers. First, Mary should try to add rooms to her life, if she can't add rooms to her house. The work of art in the honored alcove of the American development house is only too apt to be the television set. Like a Japanese family, the American family sits before its tokonoma in silence. But there the similarity ends. In the Japanese house, the tokonoma contains something the family created; something that represents the genius of the family. The family contemplates its work with pride and profit. In the American house, the picture eye in the tokonoma reflects the outside world; instead of representing the family, it represents other people's activities. It is specifically designed to turn attention outward, away from home.

In other words, if Mary is to be a happier housewife, it jolly well behooves her to turn her attention inward to see if she can't become a homemaker. She must be creative if she would find salvation. If she simply follows fads, or relies on outside advice for everything from boiling water to buying new drapes, she is well on the way to nonentity. Eve Wild was the happiest woman in Rolling Knolls because she relied on herself. She baked her own bread, painted her own pictures, and had as little to do with her neighbors as was humanly possible. She never confused her neighbors with her friends.

The Mary Drones of our developments can take a hint from Eve and the Japanese with regard to neighborly relations. Neighbors don't have to like one another to be good neighbors. A good neighbor is merely somebody ready and willing to pat you on the back if your coat catches fire. Development people, however, seem to believe that to be a good neighbor they must become intimate companions of the folks next door, just because they're the folks next door. Thus, they exchange the most shocking personal information as a matter of course and become involved with one another's emotional experiences. It is all a very trying situation, serving only to breed mutual contempt. Since the Mary Drones of our developments are fated to meet one another frequently, they might substitute a Japanese politeness for intimacy. Manners are nothing more than a device to permit people to conduct necessary, everyday relationships on an impersonal plane. On their jam-packed little islands, the Japanese have brought polite convention to the level of high art— another invention born of necessity.

Well—it's just a suggestion, probably impossible to carry out in this country today. Americans are notorious for their constant asking of direct, personal questions of one another. Even our most ordinary polite greeting, "How do you do?" is a request for specific information. And the typical Midwestern waitress who asks, the minute you sit at table,

"How are you today?" is requesting information even more specific. If developments in current production keep spreading, and the people in them keep acting the way they do, we're all either going to wind up in the looney bin or adopt a Japanese pattern of life. If we are going to live in bedroom neighborhoods, we must either accent our individualities or all go to hell in the same handbasket, and it's as simple as that.

In an homogenous community of look-alike houses peopled with act-alike neighbors of identical age groups, there's not too much we can do to improve our lot *except* accent such small discrepancies as may exist, and lock our differences within our doors to keep them safe. On the other hand, there are certain things that can be done to make the neighborhood itself more palatable, to give it the illusion of being something of a community.

If, by such a curious oversight as occurred in West Falls Church, Virginia, a tract of several acres is left undeveloped amid a welter of housing developments, a healthful opportunity presents itself. The good neighbors of the Falls Church area pooled their resources and bought the land. They've put in a swimming pool so far and plan other recreational facilities—a playing field, a picnic area with fireplaces and tables, and carefully tended woods. Their purchase has given them a common focus of interest, added variety to their lives, and has helped make their collection of houses something more than just that. If, as is most often the case, there is no adjacent land to be turned into a recreational area, development dwellers are still presented an opportunity every time a house goes up for sale in their neighborhood. They can get together to buy the house and turn it into a library or a teen-age clubhouse, or a church. If the zoning laws don't seem to permit this, the neighbors can see if they can't persuade the zoning board to bend the law a little. It's easy to do—builders do it all the time. In either event, people must spend money, but whatever price is paid, the deal will be more of a bargain than any they'll find advertised.

It is far more difficult to suggest answers to other human problems posed by our present developments. How are you going to persuade a young family it shouldn't spend money it doesn't have for things it doesn't need? Especially when the government, a little worried by fast-rising consumer credit, says it's thinking of making credit even easier than ever in order to keep sales high? You can only point out that our pressure for conformity is great, and beg young people to consider, carefully, whether they really need that revolving, electrical chicken toaster before they go in debt for it just because they're afraid that, if they don't buy one, they'll miss what the Joneses are enjoying. And how can the matriarchal aspects of developments be lessened? Only by suggesting what should be painfully clear—that fathers make every effort to spend more of such time as they have with their families. You can tell development fathers they should accept, rather than abandon to the mother, all the family responsibility they can shoulder. But here, you are on treacherous ground, if you also accept what Miss O'Malley believes to be true—that most development fathers are weak and childish, mated to so many triumphant, spouse-devouring black widows.

The reader will recall that Mary Drone sought only more space when she decided to leave Rolling Knolls. In moving to a larger house, she solved only one part of her threefold problem; the homogeneity of the neighbors and the neighborhood again sucked her back into ennui. Sensing something

Less of a matriarchy.

was wrong, she almost at once thought of moving a third
time—as soon as possible. Selling out at some future time
is the dream of nearly all development families. Like her
neighbors, Mary regarded her house, whether in Rolling
Knolls or in Merryland Dell, as a temporary expedient. In
so thinking, she hovered on the brink of a great truth. The
optimum value of a development house *is* that of a temporary
expedient. If some means could be found to make our current
developments into rental units, we might remove a great
source of nervous tension. Dwellers would no longer feel
hopelessly trapped, torn by the inadequacy of their house on
one side; rended by the knowledge they're stuck with it on
the other. They would in truth be free to move.

There is no question that the two-bedroom postwar development house has certain advantages for the very young family. Together with its tiny lot, it serves as a playpen for the diaper set. Its monthly mortgage payments seem to be (and are, if not carried on too long) cheaper than rent on an apartment of the same floor space. They are within a young family's means. If developments of such houses are slums, as Yale's Dr. Winslow says they are, they are nonetheless open-air slums, more healthful than New York City's rabbit warrens. They are more waterproof than a colony of tents and—all in all—serve a useful purpose for a short time. I do not suggest the government buy them from their current owners and administer them as rental units, because I'm crotchety enough, and long enough in the tooth, to think the government should keep its sticky little fingers out of as many pies as possible. But I do suggest that some business firm, whose every action is motivated by the best interests of the client, as Representative Broyhill would say, should gobble them up and put them on a rental basis, operating as a public utility. It seems to me that here is a ready-made investment field for insurance companies, or for one of those big, tax-free foundations dedicated to the general uplift.

In such case, the young family could rent at a modest fee until, by virtue of its own disciplines and ambitions, it is able to buy or build the house that comes closer to its dream. If it fails to achieve its ambitions . . . it fails. A certain number of our citizens now live in non-fresh-air slums. An awful lot of grass seed never germinates.

Wistful as this suggestion might seem, there are other advantages in converting our current developments into rental properties. Not only would young people be free to move when they'd outgrown the development house, but they would also be free of that boobytrap in the GI mortgage guarantee, whereby they're stuck, as was John Drone, if their subsequent purchaser defaults on the mortgage. Moreover, the government—you, the taxpayer—would be out from under walls bound to come tumbling down in event of depression.

Frankly, trying to think of ways and means to improve our developments-in-being is an appalling task, and the suggestions made here are not offered as panaceas. They are made only in the hope that you can think of better solutions. No one can deny that problems exist, and a problem exists only to be solved.

To my mind, the chief value of the development-in-being is that it provides the horrible example. It is the sin-sodden drunk, the ne'er-do-well, shambling down the village street at eleven o'clock on Sunday morning, the pity and the despair of the congregation. Brethren, it's up to us to prevent our children from falling into that wretched state. Specifically, we'll have to give a thought while yet we can, to the developments that are still a glitter in the builders' little red eyes. Maybe, as Robert Woods Kennedy says, we'll have to ram a kind of Pure Food and Drug Act down the builders' throats. Maybe we can achieve the same ends without resort to this drastic therapy. But first, let's heft the weight of the second major problem that faces us.

The most blatant facts are these: that by 1975, 75 per cent of all Americans will be living in urban areas; that many of our cities are nearing the saturation point and therefore 85 per cent of urban area growth during the next twenty years will be suburban growth.

On last March 2, *U.S. News & World Report* took a look at the shape of things to come with the aid of the U.S.

Census Bureau and area planners in New York, Chicago, Los Angeles, Philadelphia, Detroit, Boston, San Francisco, Oakland, Pittsburgh, St. Louis, Cleveland, Washington, Minneapolis, St. Paul, Cincinnati, Kansas City (Missouri), Portland (Oregon), Dallas, Louisville, Denver, Birmingham, Columbus, Rochester, Dayton, Omaha and Oklahoma City. All these metropolitan areas anticipated a growth during the next twenty years ranging from 6 per cent in Rochester to 111 per cent in Dallas. In addition, the magazine reported, Miami expects to add a quarter of a million people in the next five years, chiefly in suburban areas. In every case, each city area evaluated by the report anticipated a fantastically higher rate of suburban growth than urban growth, and two cities, Rochester and Cleveland, anticipated a decline in their urban population to be offset by suburban increases.

Stunned by these figures, *U.S. News & World Report* concluded, "The living pattern of the American people appears certain to be undergoing a basic change." A more careful understatement never saw print. It is the safest speculation in the history of American journalism.

The *Report's* skilled guessers went on to predict there'd be a brisk business in sewer pipes, water mains, fire engines, utility networks, street, highway, school, park, shop, hospital, office and filling station construction coast-to-coast over the next couple of decades.

Sounds fine, doesn't it? But, before we carry the banners reading "Business Will Be Better Than Ever" in the torchlight parade down Main Street, let's give a thought to Main Street itself.

Within the metropolitan areas, the general trend is for the middle class to rush from the city to the suburbs, leaving a vacuum in the city to be filled by the always prolific lower class. This trend, as the *Report* noted, creates some nasty tax problems. The city must still provide its same transportation, police, fire, school, welfare and other services, but without the help of the middle-class taxpayers. Indeed, with suburbs mushrooming around the edges of the town, the city must provide increased services—such as more traffic-control systems—and can only look for its funds to a population increasingly less able to pay taxes. One result is an increased tax on city businesses. But meanwhile, the businessmen are getting out of town in droves. More than anything else, stores need customers, and retail merchants have been dashing out after their prey, shifting their major operations to the development shopping centers. Casting around for urgently-needed revenue, the cities are, as the *Report* says, "resorting to tax policies that tap the pocketbooks of outside residents. Sales taxes and payroll taxes are two of the most popular measures. Some cities also impose occupancy taxes on hotel rooms and special levies on restaurant meals."

In the midst of this disturbance, the automobile provides the final spasm in the clogged civic colon. The existence of the suburban development is almost entirely dependent upon the automobile, and for that matter, the two-car family is becoming routine. He needs his car to get to work; she needs a car to get to the shopping center or as a means of escape from the horrors of development life. Perhaps both cars are driven into the city.

Not all cities are so bountifully served by commuter trains, ferries and buses as New York City, and every day, right now, our major cities are traffic-swarming nightmares from seven to nine-thirty A.M. and from four to six P.M., when the development tide flows and ebbs. What the streets will resemble twenty years from now, when the suburbs have increased another 85 per cent, is something too hideous to contemplate. Los Angeles, a vast, smog-shrouded slum in Southern California, has four million cars today, and the average commuting time is one and one half hours. One luckless local figures he sits half an hour every morning in his driveway, foot on the clutch, engine idling fast, waiting for a chance to scuttle into a hole in the traffic. And Los Angeles anticipates a 145 per cent increase in its suburban growth in the next twenty years.

Many business and manufacturing firms are aware that traffic-packed streets are costing them money. Their personnel men are now figuring the man-hours lost (in terms of consumed energy) by the commuting employees who arrive at the time clock spent and blowing from their fight with the traffic. The firms are beginning to move out of town, too, and this again takes tax money out of the hard-pressed cities.

If we permit our cities and suburbs to continue to grow like Topsy, we're merely going to enlarge the kind of metropolitan cesspool which already offends the nose, the eye, the ear and the mind. E. A. Gutkind, in his book *The Expanding Environment,* accurately says that in our metropolitan areas "the last vestiges of a community have disappeared. They are hardly anything else than an agglomeration of innumerable and isolated details, of human atoms and rows of boxes, called houses, interspersed between the industries. It is a total victory of a laissez-faire insensibility and recklessness over organic growth and even over organized development. Our towns are work-centered power stations of the National State. They are inhabited by human automata and they deliver the vast army of Experts, the grave diggers of our civilization . . .

"Like the Greek polis, these towns grow by accretion. But

what a difference! In Greece, certainty of social awareness restricts the size of the towns. In our western civilization, speculators' and contractors' gains are the driving power behind the unlimited growth of the cities. Extension, not limitation; uniformity, not unity in diversity, are our contribution to urban culture. Our cities exist in a spiritual and physical void."

Growth by accretion! First the work center, then the town around it. Then the drift of workers, industry and business to the suburbs; then new industry on the edge of the suburbs and new suburbs to supply the work force for the new industry; then the shift of industry and business out once

". . . a total victory of a laissez-faire insensibility . . ."

again, and on and on and on in concentric circles until you wind up with something that looks and smells like Chicago, rotten at the core. This is the pattern of our expanding environment in these years of Our Lord's Grace.

But we see our danger. Unrestricted development construction plays hob with the mental health of the individual, prevents establishment of human communities, and makes a chaos of both city and country. It is only too clear that we must put a stop to this nonsense. Grow, we must, for our population is increasing. But plan we must, before we grow into Mongolian idiots, inexorably shaped by the shape of our dwellings. Where shall we begin to plan? Well . . . let's go back to the basic human unit, the family, and consider that it lives in a house. First, what must we demand of our houses?

Happily enough, it occurred to Mr. Albert M. Cole, as Federal Housing Administrator, to put this question to America's housewives. The fact that he asked it last April is proof—if any is needed—that a vast number of houses built under FHA auspices were just plain lousy.

"In the decade ahead," Mr. Cole said, "the American people will invest at least another $100 billion in new homes. The government does not propose to be a partner to a $100-billion mistake."

Snide voters might have suggested Mr. Cole meant to say "another $100-billion mistake," but this would have been idle carping. Mr. Cole's appeal for housewifely advice was a step in the right direction, and, during April, his "American Congress of Housewives" trooped to Washington to give Mr. Cole the benefit of their advice. Nearly all of it was sound, and all of it was an illuminating indictment of our present housing mess.

The ladies wanted more closets; they wanted much more space.

"What we want," one group said, "is more storage space than you can imagine—in the attic, in the basement, the garage. So much until you might wonder what is going to happen under the bed."

"We want," another group said, "to put the whole family at the table as a family unit. Our feeling is to preserve the family as a unit where they can gather about the table in a place of serenity."

Therefore, they requested separate dining rooms instead of those tiny dinettes off the kitchen. A dining room, they said, provided parents with a room where they "could teach children good manners graciously in a quiet atmosphere."

They wanted basements and garages. They complained of look-alike monotony. They wanted the builders to leave trees on the property, and they wanted the builders to be compelled to sod the grounds as a part of the contract.

Then, and this will come as a horrid shock to the manufacturers, advertisers and salesmen of our electrical widgets, the ladies were unanimously ready to do without the gadgets if they could please have a little more space for their money.

"Comfortable living is most essential," one spokeslady told Mr. Cole. "We are most interested in getting rid of the froufrou. We don't want too many built-in gadgets. Out with the wall ovens and air conditioners!"

Mr. Cole asked the ladies to think in terms of a $10,000 house. As it turned out, the ladies' dream house would cost $20,000 on today's metropolitan market. After relentless pruning and compromising, one Midwestern group offered their absolute minimum requirements, and to build the house of their interrupted dream would cost $14,500 on the current market. Still, many ladies said they were willing to pay for it. The house of their dreams, curiously enough, turned out to bear a striking resemblance to that old family house on Elm Street.

Mr. Cole is to be congratulated for asking the ladies what they'd like in a house, and it's the kind of question that will make him a popular fellow. More important, the answers he received may well find their ways into future FHA regulations. At this point, Mr. Cole would be well advised to call a Congress of the nation's architects—a group of men I conceive to have been shouting in a wilderness for much too long a time.

Architects understand as well or better than Mama what Mama wants in her house, because relating the house to the needs of the inhabitants has always been the first science of their profession. They've studied the matter for centuries. It should surprise no one to learn that many developments were spawned by builders who simply followed a general floor plan snipped out of a magazine, or, in other instances, relied on their own pea-sized brains for inspiration, and built gadgets rather than houses and marketed them like gadgets. The split-level idea is merely a means of packaging a gadget. Other builders hired an architect on the following terms: Tell me how cheap I can build a house. Then, armed with the resulting minimum plan, the builder repeated himself five hundred times and called it a development. The needs of the inhabitants were given the most fleeting, derisive glance by builders whose entire attention was centered on making money. But a house, as Frank Lloyd Wright says, "should be in the character of a work of art instead of being simply a property to be traded in."

Surely Mr. Cole will find many answers to his question in

Robert Woods Kennedy's majestic book, *The House.* Mr.
Kennedy is almost entirely preoccupied by thoughts of the
people who must live in a house. What do people do indoors?
How much space do their various activities require? How
much time is devoted to any particular activity? Where do
their normal movements lead them through the house? What
are their esthetic needs and how are these to be met?
What are the individual needs of each member of the family
and how can a house satisfy them? Mr. Kennedy considers
these matters at length.

The American housewife, Mr. Kennedy suggests, is ideally
expected to be a household drudge, a vision of delight, an
accomplished courtesan, a loving teacher of the young, a
social ornament and an intellectual partner. Instead of
assisting her to achieve this admirable combination of attri-
butes, the houses in current production, Mr. Kennedy suggests, are more apt to turn her into a dull-witted, nagging
slob. Likewise, the familiar box on the slab contributes
toward the father's becoming a woman-bossed, inadequate,
money-terrified neuter, instead of helping him to accomplish
the American dream of the male: rich, handsome, famous,
masterful, and the dispenser of even-handed justice. Instead
of either stifling the child or forcing him to seek his pleasures
elsewhere, a house should fit the child's energetic needs, give
him plenty of space, and later, when he hits the teens, afford
him decent privacy wherein to entertain his contemporaries.
In other words, Mr. Kennedy completely understands that a
dwelling shapes the dweller, and he, as an architect, has
studied the effects of various dwelling shapes on people.

Therefore, Mr. Kennedy asks each family to consider how
much of its time, thought and energy is spent on excreting,
sleeping and love-making, cooking, eating, working and

having fun. Once these facts are known, and viewpoints of the individuals are heard, and their personalities understood, the architect can begin to consider the bathroom, bedroom, kitchen, dining room, study and living room, and assemble specific ideas on paper. He can plot out the shape of each area of use and figure out the most practical traffic patterns among these areas, keeping the site of the house always in mind. You don't, ideally, simply dump a house down in the middle of a lot. Instead, you fit the house to its site, for the shape of the site is critically important.

"To change every contour of a site is not only to strip it of every precious root, tree and flower," Mr. Kennedy says. "It is to make an enemy of it. When sites are so violated, their injured subsurface drainage patterns break out in the form of leaking basements, and their mangled topsoil departs with wind and water. The 'touch not a hair of yon grey head' motto is often more successful. But in its negation of man's impact, it is equally unbalanced. The skillfully blended contour road; the straight double row of trees, the geometric or free patterning of areas, emphasize the connection between the site's natural patterns and the human uses imposed. This sort of contrast is one sort of esthetic pleasure. Another, depending on synthesis rather than contrast, is the realization that the finite site is related to the ethos of its region's landscape . . . The ethos in question here is like the atmosphere of a marriage. It is invisible, over and above the two parties concerned, yet inseparable from them. The good designer regards site and building in the same light."

Therefore, building materials or the color of the paint, also blend with the site, and the site with its region.

Every word of Mr. Kennedy's book sounds damned expensive to the home purchaser, and—of course—it is, because

Mr. Kennedy is primarily interested in building individual houses for individuals.

It is idle to pretend everyone can hire his own architect and build his own mansion. Mr. Kennedy's thoughts are presented here only as an ideal. Nevertheless, we can make some attempts to approach his goal. All too many families buy a box on a slab just because it is the cheapest thing they can find closest to father's work. One Maryland family was presented with a choice—a $10,000 two-bedroom box in a development close to Washington, or an older, $10,000 four-bedroom house with living room, dining room, farm kitchen, front and back porches, full basement, attic, two-car garage and half an acre of lawns and trees thirty miles from the city. Thinking only of the commuting, they took the box and have been kicking themselves ever since. Their pangs are all the more sharp because another man, who worked in the same downtown office, bought the country house and claimed the commuting was no problem. He said it was more than over-balanced by the advantages his family derived from the space it enjoyed. Obviously, the solution found here—driving sixty miles each day to and from work—is not one many people would think practical. We must find better answers than a residence in the boondocks.

We can, therefore, follow Mr. Kennedy's advice insofar as we are able, by thinking first what each person in the family requires of a house, and seeking a residence that presents maximum space best suited to the areas of maximum use—then reconciling these matters with the asking price and other factors. Other factors? Yes, lots of other factors, such as water supply, utilities, public transportation, local school system, fire protection, crime rate, proximity to hospitals, shops, recreational areas and cultural facilities. It is a big equation with lots of factors, but the most important factor of all is the one today's builders have ignored—the family. The people who live in the house.

Mr. Cole, having put his question to the ladies, can turn to men like Mr. Kennedy for help in drafting specific, practical changes in the FHA building regulations. Mr. Cole's ladies have done the pure theory work in their home laboratories. Mr. Kennedy and his fellow architects are familiar with the theory, and they're the only trained engineers we have to figure out how to put the theory into practice. Surely, a nation that produced the atomic bomb can devise some way to build an adequate house at a reasonable price. In our era of wonders, perhaps our architects can figure a way to build a spacious house out of ten cents' worth of a rotproof, bugproof, fast-color plastic ten times stronger than steel, simply by adding water and stirring. One thing *is* certain: twenty years of suburban expansion lie ahead, and if we keep on building Merryland Dells and Rolling Knolls Estates we'll have no one to blame but ourselves. We must start building real houses for living people, and at a price we can afford. If we must, we can.

Proper design of a single house is not an entire answer, by any means. The big equation is composed of all those other factors. We are going to have to relate the adequate house of our future to the community in which it will stand. Unless we're going to be content with a simple widening of Mr. Gutkind's metropolitan accretion, it looks very much as though we'll have to do a little practical planning. Richard Neutra, in *Survival Through Design*, puts the case thus:

"Man's own cramped-together creations, anything from underground sewage systems and subways to a badly hemmed-in sky overhead, irritatingly crisscrossed by a maze of electric wires, should not prove inescapable as fate. Lightning and the plague, once so formidable, have been countered by proper measures; must we then and here find ourselves helpless? Must we remain victims, strangled and suffocated by our own design which has surrounded us with man-devouring metropolises, drab small towns manifesting a lack of order devastating to the soul, blighted countrysides along railroad tracks and highways, studded with petty 'mere utility' structures, shaded by telephone poles and scented by gasoline fumes?"

The answer to this rhetoric should be a rousing No. Meanwhile, Mr. Neutra plunges on to suggest that there's not much we can do to improve the messes we've made to date.

"Factories," he said, "railway depots, office buildings, cheap mass-housing schemes and city plans which were first thrown together or engineered for utility and then dressed up for beauty demonstrate daily that they have painfully little kinship to life and in fact are fairly foreign to it. They cannot really sustain it."

Perhaps Mr. Neutra might agree with men like Clarence Stein, who seriously suggest we pull down our towns and begin all over again—a proposition that would surely guarantee everyone in the nation a living wage for years to come. At any rate, Mr. Stein, one of our top-drawer planners, says, "in the formless city of the present, community life and face-to-face democracy has [sic] been submerged and lost. New communities should be small enough to permit neighborliness and participation of all members in common concerns, but large enough to allow a rich and varied community life and to support adequate communal facilities economically."

He believes we should create small neighborhoods based

on grammar school populations; neighborhoods small enough to permit each individual to play a personal role in community life.

Next, he would limit the growth of urban areas to preserve neighborhood and city political identity, with sharply defined boundaries. If the boundaries are natural, so much the better.

Third, Mr. Stein would group neighborhoods in such a way as to enable them to acquire for joint use facilities such as large hospitals, high schools, professional theaters and so on—facilities which no small neighborhood could adequately support.

Fourth, Mr. Stein's regional city complex would be made up of a constellation of small towns bound together by "townless" superhighway networks. The roads wouldn't go through town—you'd get on them via cloverleaves, as on our big Eastern toll roads.

Fifth, each neighborhood district and town would be so planned as to focus on its own community center.

To Mr. Stein's way of thinking, the zoning and planning of unbuilt areas would not be concerned so much with the shape and size of house lots as with developing self-contained communities which, in the sociological sense, answer the needs of the inhabitants. Thus, Mr. Stein's block pattern is more important than the lot pattern, and the shape of the neighborhood more important than the shape of the block. He dreams of a world where there is separation of pedestrian and vehicular traffic, centrally located shopping and recreational areas within walking distance of every home.

This might sound a little like a science-fiction writer's dream of a brave new world of decentralized industries and town complexes built radially from work centers, each distant from the other, but joined by a spider web of roads. But wait—think again. Doesn't it also sound a little like a shape this nation once knew? Doesn't it recall a countryside studded here and there with small, self-sufficient and individualistic towns? This plan surely soothes some of the anguish felt by Thomas Sharp, who in *Town and Country-side* lamented:

> Two diametrically opposed, diametrically contrasting, inevitable types of beauty are being displaced by one drab, revolting, neutrality. Rural influences neutralize the town. Urban influences neutralize the country. In a few years, all will be neutrality. The strong, masculine virility of the town; the softer beauty, the richness, the fruitfulness of that mother of men, the countryside, will be debased into one sterile, hermaphroditic beastliness.
>
> The crying need of the moment is the re-establishment of the ancient antithesis. The town is town: the country is country: black and white: male and female. Only in the preservation of these distinctions is there any salvation: only through the preservation of the town as town can the countryside be saved; and only through the limitation of rurality to the country can the town be preserved.

Of course Mr. Sharp is a confessed black-or-whiter. While he might be content to live in a cement city that stops abruptly at the edge of a cow pasture, everyone is not so attuned. We are making constant efforts to bring something of the country into our cities, because we, being land animals and children of nature, very badly need something of that soft, rich, fruitful mother of men about us. Let's just make sure the labor doesn't produce Mr. Sharp's beastly hermaphrodite.

This being a country where people may govern themselves

if they only work at it, we can, in our local communities, draw up any zoning laws and building regulations we wish. We should, in our town and city councils, ask ourselves how many dwelling units are currently available, what is their age and condition, what is our present and anticipated population, and what is our housing demand. These facts are no farther away than the local courthouse files.

Assume we've rooted through the files and have the facts. The area is going to grow by X people and most likely in Y direction, and meanwhile, there will be Z work to do in the center of town. What should we do, and how should we do it? Fortunately, the best advice of the world's public and private planners, traffic engineers and architects is always available. It is no farther away than the local library. A person who offers advice may be a fool, but a person who does not listen to advice to see whether he can use any part of it is the north end of a southbound horse. Therefore, we study what other men have thought, what other communities have done, and then begin to work out our own approaches to our problems. In so doing, we function as a zoning board and as a board on building regulations.

As a zoning board, we get together to agree that here we will have a school; there a business area; this place will be set aside for recreational use; we will permit construction of rental units here; private residences there, and so on. We have the vision of our future community in mind. As a zoning board, we will also keep in mind that the designers of a site plan, by deciding where the streets will go and how the houses will face, and how much land is to be left between houses, are also determining the pattern of the community's social life. If ours is a metropolitan community, we'll need a regional master zoning plan. It is not always an answer for a city simply to reach out and annex its suburbs, hoping thereby to answer either a tax problem or to bring a large area into one political structure for administrative convenience. Only too often the result is civic indigestion in trying to keep down two different kinds of problems. Only too often are the interests of either city or suburbs submerged in a total vote. It is better to keep our politics on what Washington calls "the local level."

When we function as a building regulation board, we can pass any kind of regulations we see fit—and make them stick. We can, like Scarsdale, New York, ban monotonous development by prohibiting builders from slapping up look-alike boxes; by requiring each house to be substantially different from its neighbor. As a building board, we have the monstrous responsibility of creating the intimate pattern of family life to be led in the houses to be built. If we permit builders to continue to throw up Rolling Knolls Estates, we are going to create social and mental illness in our home towns. Therefore, we can set our building standards high, secure in the knowledge that builders will simply have to meet them or not build. Don't think they'll stop building. They want to stay in business, so they'll meet the standards. They will also price their houses within our means if they wish to sell them. They'll either develop more efficient construction methods, leave out the meaningless frills, or shave their profits. Today's development houses are uniformly substandard and overpriced in all price brackets. We can help cut the price by putting ceilings on land values, ending the current kiting that permits builders to boast, "We sell the land and give the house away." I am not ordinarily in favor of government controls and sometimes think creation of the federal post office was a step in the wrong direction, but I recognize the fact there are public utilities, and I think housing is a public utility. To my mind, construction firms could properly be brought within the jurisdiction of a public utilities commission and be assigned a certain percentage of profit on their capital investments, just as are gas, electric power and transportation systems. I am not suggesting the government should enter the housing business—my memories of the federally-built slum of Oak Ridge are only too vivid. I suggest that we, in our local communities, can set our own standards.

No specific recommendations will be given here for you to follow, because problems differ in detail from locality to locality across the nation. In some areas, there is much time for careful consideration. Loudon County, Virginia, in theoretical commuting range of Washington, acted before theory was translated into fact. Horrified by what had happened in Arlington and Fairfax counties, near-by Loudon delivered itself of zoning regulations that flatly ban construction of housing developments. Metropolitan areas already bursting their buttons do not have Loudon's leisure—their problems are here and now. But there is still not the same urgency to build much and fast as there was at the end of World War II, and even the most crowded metropolitan areas can make time to think. It might be a temporary hardship on an appreciable number of people if a big city suddenly canceled all building permits and refused to grant new permits until it set up a master zoning plan. But consider the permanent damage to hundreds of thousands of people when development is unrestricted.

The point is, as long as we have representative government, we can make our own terms. Or, if we prefer, we can just laze back and take whatever the builders hand us. In that case, we'll get just what we deserve, as did the citizens of Montgomery County, Maryland.

Some years ago, a Montgomery County council hired experts to make a master zoning plan for upper county development. The planners decided to cut the land up into agricultural, country home, residential, commercial and industrial areas to protect the county's economic stability. Particularly, they were interested in preserving the rich dairy industry as a stabilizing influence, and to limit the spread of the kind of box-on-a-slab development that had already begun to pose serious questions in the down-county area adjacent to Washington. Under their plans, farmers would find it impossible to sell their land to developers. They couldn't even sell small bits of it for individual building sites. Naturally, all this brought immediate shrieks from the real-estate element. The plan had not been adopted when election time rolled around and a new county council came in.

The new council, dominated by members in real-estate businesses, appeared dedicated to the proposition that the county's master zoning plan would vanish from this earth. They tossed it aside and brought in a planner of their own, thinking he might hatch schemes closer to their hearts, which they carried in their back pockets. Unfortunately for the new council, the man they hired came up with nearly the same proposals as the original planners. Angrily, the council spiked his plan.

Meanwhile, a series of meetings had been held throughout the upper county, with the planners explaining their side of things, and the real-estate boys showing up to shout theirs. Neither planners nor the real-estate element did well on an intellectual basis. Too often the planners wound up talking about preserving the beauty of the countryside while just as often their opponents were saying the plan was intended to deprive the poor dirt farmer of his God-given right to do what he damn well pleased with his own land. Nobody, particularly the real-estate crowd, mentioned the community's right to plan land use on some rational basis. Probably the planners thought the point so elementary it needed no mentioning, and the real-estate types found it one bit of scripture they couldn't quote to their own purpose.

You might think the question—which really boiled down to whether the farm area would be opened to unrestricted development—would have whipped the citizenry up into some degree of lather, inasmuch as they were being asked to consider their own future. For instance, you might have thought the farmers would be interested, if no one else. But the *Montgomery County Sentinel* proved otherwise. The newspaper sent out 12,000 blanks to sample public opinion on the zoning propositions, and exactly 120 people bothered to fill them out and send them back. Opinion was evenly divided. Since one half of one per cent of an electorate never frightened a politician, there are now signs reading "BUILD-ING SITES FOR SALE" dotting the up-county farms. In the normal course of things, you can expect Montgomery County to become another giant clutter of slapdash match-boxes, all alike, all jammed together, lumpy with shopping centers and boiling with public and private tensions, just like all other county areas adjacent to Washington.

Mr. Frederick A. Gutheim, county resident and nationally-known planning consultant, held a post mortem. The zoning plans were defeated, he said, "by a planned campaign of delays, misrepresentations and protests organized by a small group of self-interested land speculators, real-estate brokers, home builders and small-minded Democratic machine politicians." The campaign succeeded only because nobody except that ill-met crew allowed themselves to become interested. It was a wild victory for apathy.

The central lesson here is that at all times the land agents and builders are thinking in specific terms, constantly pressing for their own ends, and if you ever step down from the barricades, or never mount them, you'll find the bulldozers busy among the trees before you can say cash. In all fairness, we must not believe all builders are cynical and contemptuous of the public good. Many are kind to their aged mothers, thoughtful of their young, and some would not filch pennies from the eyes of the dead. They just haven't been told how to behave, and their innocent enthusiasms often result in public tragedies.

More insidious and far more dangerous than any other influence, is the housing development's destruction of individuality. We live in a time of mass terms. Poll-takers feel the mass pulse, merchants angle for mass markets, products are mass-produced, schools offer mass education, our communications are mass media and we're constantly being badgered to look around us and make sure we're doing and saying and thinking what the mass of our neighbors will accept. The closer we huddle together, the greater this pressure for conformity becomes, and today's housing development gives impetus to this pressure in every way. The physically monotonous development of mass houses is a leveling influence in itself, breeding swarms of neuter drones.

I submit, as proved, that these drones are prey to drift and abyssal boredom, and cannot be said to have lives of their own. I submit housing developments combine the worst disadvantages of suburbs and city slums without reflecting the advantages of either. I submit housing developments are a disruptive influence in our national life. I submit housing developments pose many clear and present dangers to us all, and on that thought, conclude this inquest.

You, members of the coroner's jury, will now retire to consider your verdict, for as in any democratic court, the sole power is in your hands.

Bibliography

THE SCHOLARLY reader who wishes to bog himself down with further researches into development life, its origins, delights and despairs, might find the following source material helpful:

All housing articles published between 1947 and 1955 in the pages of the *New York Times* and the *Washington Star*.

All housing articles published between 1947 and 1955 in the following magazines: *American City, American Journal of Sociology, American Journal of Public Health, Business Week, Collier's, Commonweal, Fortune, Harper's, Monthly Labor Review, The New Republic, The Reporter, The Saturday Evening Post, Scientific Monthly, U.S. News & World Report*.

An excellent study in national housing frustration is House Report No. 2501, 2d session, 82d Congress, September 11, 1952.

The following books are even more helpful:

Carr, Lowell Julliard, and Stermer, Edson, *Willow Run*. New York, Harper Bros., 1952.

Dahir, James, *The Neighborhood Unit Plan*, a bibliography. New York, Russell Sage Foundation, 1947.

Eckbo, Garrett, *Landscape for Living*. Duell, Sloan & Pearce, 1950.

Festinger, Schachter and Back, *Social Pressures in Informal Groups*. New York, Harper Bros., 1950.

Gutkind, E. A., *Community and Environment*. London, Watts & Co., 1953.

―――― *The Expanding Environment*. London, Freedom Press, 1953.

Kennedy, Robert Woods, *The House and the Art of Its Design*. New York, Reinhold, 1953.

Kuper, Leo, *et al.*, *Living in Towns*. London, The Cresset Press, 1953.

Neutra, Richard, *Survival Through Design*. New York, Oxford University Press, 1954.

Richards, J. M., *The Castle on the Ground*. London, The Architectural Press, 1946.

Sharp, Thomas, *Town and Countryside*. London, Oxford University Press, 1932.